Loss, Love and Lessons Learned

Loss, Love and Lessons Learned

The Story of Willy and Esther

Ervi Farkas

Full Court Press
Englewood Cliffs, New Jersey

First Edition

Copyright © 2023 by Ervi Farkas

All rights reserved. No part of this book may be reproduced or transmitted in any form or by any means electronic or mechanical, including by photocopying, by recording, or by any information storage and retrieval system, without the express permission of the author, except where permitted by law.

Published in the United States of America
by Full Court Press, 601 Palisade Avenue,
Englewood Cliffs, NJ 07632
fullcourtpress.com

ISBN 978-1-953728-16-6
Library of Congress Control No. 2023904962

Editing by Jay Schreiber

Final editing and book design by Barry Sheinkopf

Cover and interior photographs courtesy of the author

THIS BOOK IS DEDICATED TO

*Sienna Wynn, Zachary William, Ruby Eve and Zoe Esther
and the generations that will come from them,*

AND IN LOVING MEMORY OF MY PARENTS

Willy and Esther Farkas

"There are only two lasting bequests we can hope to give our children. One of these is roots, the other, wings."

—W. Hodding Carter Jr.

Table of Contents

Introduction, i

Chapter 1: Vilyatana: Where It All Started, *1*

Chapter 2: My Mother's Family Leaves Vilyatana, *11*

Chapter 3: My Father's Family Leaves Vilyatana, *24*

Chapter 4: From Ghetto to Death Camps, *31*

Chapter 5: After the War, *45*

Chapter 6: The Move to America, *59*

Chapter 7: The House in Queens (1967–2018), *92*

Chapter 8: Life with Sue, *107*

Chapter 9: Elissa and Eric and Grandchildren, *129*

Chapter 10: Simchas and Sickness, *146*

Chapter 11: Lessons Learned, *160*

Coda, *172*

Appendix A: Maps of Ukraine and Transcarpathia, 177

Appendix B: Farkas Family Tree, 178

Appendix C: Sobel Family Tree, 179

Appendix D: Davidovic Family Tree, 180

Appendix E: Eulogies for Wilhelm Farkas, 181

Appendix F: Eulogies for Esther Farkas, 195

Bibliography, 209

Acknowledgments, 211

Introduction

I am writing this book for our children, grandchildren and future generations so they may learn, as much as is possible, where they come from. It is meant to inform them of the strength, courage and grace of my parents, Wilhelm Farkas and Esther Farkas, née Davidovic, as well as others in the family who faced unbelievable hardships, losses and brutality while living through the Holocaust. In the face of this horror, they displayed astounding resilience and went on to fully embrace life in the decades that followed.

I have always said that the most important event in my life occurred in the decade before I was born. The Holocaust profoundly impacted my parents, grandparents and everyone else in the Farkas/Davidovic families as well as millions of other Jews throughout Europe, especially Eastern Europe. I will try to portray what happened--in part from family stories that were told to me or that I overheard, and in part from various readings and research I have done.

My parents rarely brought up the Holocaust when I was growing up. The losses they suffered were too much for them to deal with and certainly not something they could discuss with their children. They wanted to protect us and not burden us with what they suffered. However, when they were with friends and family who also survived the Holocaust, they spoke about the various things they went through as well as their early lives before the Holocaust. I would quietly listen and sometimes be amazed by what I was hearing. At other times, I would be aghast. In April 1979, I interviewed and audiotaped my grandfather, Samuel Farkas. My parents were videotaped for the Shoah Foundation on June 24, 1996. My uncle Moishe was also interviewed by the Shoah Foundation on December 3, 1996. In addition, while researching the family stories I recalled from when I was younger, I was able to find some records in various Holocaust museums and through other sources as well. Since my parents and grandparents are no longer alive, I feel it is my duty to tell their stories. The Holocaust was an intensely traumatic event in their lives, and it was forever part of who they were and even part of who I am. It did not define them, and it does not define me, but it inevitably shaped us, as you are about to read.

I

VILYATANA: WHERE IT ALL STARTED

MY PARENTS WERE BORN in Vilyatana (Yiddish pronunciation), which at the time of their respective births was part of Czechoslovakia. Vilyatana (Vilatyn in Ukraine) is part of Transcarpathia (see Appendix A). Transcarpathia (also called Carpathian Ruthiana) is a border region that changed countries five times during the 20th century. It was part of the Austro-Hungarian Empire before 1920. From 1920 to 1938, it was part of Czechoslovakia. In 1938, it was returned to Hungary, and in 1944, it was attached to the Soviet Union as a frontier area of the Ukraine. It is now part of Ukraine. It has been said that someone could have been born in Austria-Hungary, married in Czechoslovakia, had a child in Hungary, lived and raised a family in the Soviet Union and gone on to live in Ukraine without ever leaving the town where he or she was born.

Lying south of the Carpathian Mountains, Transcarpathia was somewhat isolated geographically and politically from other ethnically Ukrainian lands. Transcarpathia borders Romania to the south, Hungary to the southwest, Slovakia to the west and Poland to the north. The region, along the Carpathian Mountains, covers an area of almost 13,000 square kilometers of beautiful, dense, lush-green, tree-covered terrain. The mountains are intersected by river valleys with fertile plains. The high mountains are snow-covered during the winter and filled with colorful wildflowers in the summer.

In the past, the area covered the counties of Ung, Bereg, Ugocsa and Maramoros. Vilyatana is now part of the Ugocsa district and Maramoros province. It is about five miles southeast of Khust, which is the closest big town or city. There is not much written about Vilyatana, but there is a great deal written about Munkacz, which is also in the region. In fact, my parents and many of their friends were part of the Bereg Munkaczer Society during their adult lives in the United States. The society bought the plots where many of them are now buried in Wellwood Cemetery in Long Island. My father was the society's treasurer for many years, and his best friend, Joe Spiegel, was president. Unfortunately, the Bereg Munkaczer Society was liquidated recently due to the deaths of its members. But what it represented should not be forgotten. Indeed, when I visit my parents' graves, I feel my heritage and history because the graves of my grandparents, other family members and many family friends are all there as well. Almost all of them were survivors of the Holocaust, and it is fitting that they are together now, for it honors where they were born and how they were raised and completes the circle of their lives.

For my parents and other family members that circle began in Vilyatana. Vilyatana was a *shtetl*—a town or a village with a large, observant, Ashkenazi Jewish community. Ashkenazi Jews originally lived in Germany and France before they migrated eastward to countries like Hungary, Poland, Lithuania, and Russia. My four grandparents and most of my great-grandparents and great-great-grandparents were from Vilyatana. As far as I can tell, our families were already in Vilyatana in the mid to late 19th century. They may have been there earlier, but records that I was able to find on the My Jewish Heritage website do not go back beyond that point.

Marriages were arranged by the parents of other families that knew each other— acquaintances from either Vilyatana or from a neighboring town. As a result, children grew up with large extended families close by. Families usually had at least two children, but often more than that. In fact, all my grandparents had between five and nine siblings, and my great-grandfather's sister had at least 16 children. It wasn't unusual for a daughter and her mother to be pregnant at the same time. The families also followed Orthodox tradition and kept a close watch on all the children. I can recall my mother talking about seeing her aunts, uncles and grandparents when she was growing up in Vilyatana and that you couldn't do anything wrong because even if your parents were not around, some other relative would notice and make sure you behaved.

My father's family left Vilyatana when he was about 3 years old, so he didn't remember it the way my mother did. What he remembered far better was Velky Berezny, the town his family moved to. Velky Berezny (or Nagy Berezny) is also in Transcarpathia, to the north. The majority of the population in the region were Ruthenians, who were Greek Catholics and Greek Orthodox (Eastern Orthodox or Orthodox Catholic, not necessarily Greek). Historically, they were affiliated with different nationalities; some saw themselves as Russians, while others professed Ukrainian identity. The area was also home to Magyars (ethnic Hungarians), Jews, Slovaks, Romanians, Czechs, Poles and Roma (or Gypsies).

The Jews in the Transcarpathian region adhered closely to their religious traditions, in contrast to Hungarian Jews, who were inclined to assimilate into the larger Hungarian culture in which they found themselves. In 1930, more than 90 percent of Transcarpathian Jews considered themselves Jews by nationality. The rabbis' authority in these communities was supreme and considered law. Many Hasidic sects arose in the area, including in Munkacz, Szatmar, Belz and several other places.

The first significant migration of Jews to the area came after the Chmielnicki pogroms of 1648–1649, when the Cossacks in Ukraine systematically attacked and massacred Jews. Due to the region's lack of raw materials, there was little to no industrial development. The labor force, including Jews, was composed primarily of farmers, artisans, lumberjacks, oarsmen who guided logs down the rivers, peddlers and wagoneers. There were also some manufacturers and vendors of alcoholic beverages. Some Jews made a living in religious posts—they were rabbis, rabbinical court judges, ritual slaughterers (*shochets*) and teachers in *cheders* (Jewish schools). Most of the Jews were poor, regardless of how they made their living, with only a small number enjoying affluence. Almost all of them, rich or poor, spoke Yiddish. In contrast to other areas of Ukraine, Transcarpathia did not experience numerous riots and pogroms targeted towards Jews.

The Farkas Tree: Paternal Grandfather and Maternal Grandmother

Wilhelm Farkas, my father, was born on Yom Kippur, September 18, 1926. He was the third of seven children born to Samuel

Farkas and Brana Farkas *née* Sobel. My mother, Esther Farkas *née* Davidovic, was born August 10, 1929. She was the first child born to Efraim Davidovic and Barbara (Bruchela) Davidovic *née* Farkas.

The fact that the name Farkas appears on both sides of my family tree in the previous sentence is not a mistake. My parents were first cousins because my father's father and my mother's mother were brother and sister. My father's father was nine years older than his sister and considerably more learned and was very revered by her. He was thought of as the head of the family when I was growing up.

My mother and her siblings always referred to my paternal grandfather (Samuel Farkas) as "*der uncle.*" While my maternal grandmother (Barbara Davidovic) was my father's aunt, he always referred to her as "*der mama,*" especially after she came to live with us after my maternal grandfather died in 1970. Elissa and Eric, our children, called my grandfather "Old Zeide" because they called my father "Zeide". My grandmother was always "Babi" to all of us.

Samuel Farkas, who was born on January 23, 1898, was the fourth of nine children born to Wolf (Smila) Farkas and Pava Farkas *née* Mozses. My maternal grandmother, Barbara (Brochula), was their ninth child. Both parents were born in Vilyatana. Wolf Farkas' parents were Soloman and Sarah Farkas. When Soloman died at a relatively young age, Sarah Farkas married Hershel, whose last name is unknown to me. He was called "*Fetter Hershel*" (Uncle Hershel) by my parents. Wolf Farkas left and went to Poland when he was a teenager to learn how to be a lumberman. He spent a few years acquiring the various skills needed for such work and became very good at it. As a result, he was able to find work in the Carpathian Mountains.

Pava Farkas' parents were Shlomo Yosef Moszes (Moses) and Esther Moszes *née* Shlomovitch. My grandfather noted Esther had one leg but was "very well-learned and religious." The Baba Esther, as she was called, died at age 91, in or around 1914. This meant she was born in Vilyatana in the mid to late 1820s. She came from a family with some wealth that was able to give Shlomo and Esther some land. The land was used to grow a garden with vegetables and flowers. Pava Farkas was very young—14, I think—when her marriage to Wolf was arranged. As for Wolf Farkas, being a lumberman meant being away from the family to work in the Carpathian Mountains. He was gone for a week at a time, or sometimes several weeks. He set up a small general store to provide additional income when he was not working in the woods and for his wife to run when he was away. During one of his weekly trips to town on his wagon, he had an accident—perhaps the wagon fell over—and it left him disabled. He then died from the accident several months later. Pava continued to run the small store after his death.

The oldest of Wolf and Pava Farkas' children was Sarah (born 1890) and she, in turn, had seven children. Her husband was also a Farkas but not related. He, too, had a store.

Sarah and five of her children died in 1944 when they were taken to Auschwitz. Two of her children, Avrum Grunbaum and Tzaler Farkas, survived the war and were living in Brooklyn when my parents and I came to the United States in 1952. Tzaler married Malka (Tanta Malchy), and they had two children, Moshe Shmiel and Suri. They were a few years older than me, and I can recall playing the Chutes and Ladders and Candy Land board games with them when we lived in Williamsburg from 1953 to 1958, and also collecting coins and stamps together. My uncle Avrum married Olga Rosenthal. I used to sleep over at their house (in Williamsburg and later in Borough Park) every once in a while, as they did not have children. If you're wondering how my uncle Avrum became Avrum Grunbaum, it turns out that he had lung issues and was unable to obtain permission to emigrate to the United States. As a result, he bought the certificates he needed to get into the United States from somebody named Grunbaum.

Avrum was religious and very astute when it came to running a business. He was involved along with Tzaler in the Mehadrin Dairy Company, which made *glatt* kosher dairy products. He also owned a nursing home in Queens (the New Glen Oaks Nursing Home), where my mother worked as a dietician for many years until she retired. I used to work there on Sundays as well to make some extra money when I was in college. While Avrum and Tzaler were ultra-Orthodox, they were not Hasidim. Their children, however, became Satmar Hasidim. Even though I grew up with them and loved playing with them when we were children in Williamsburg, as adults, we only saw one another at funerals, and so, unfortunately, we have basically lost touch.

Wolf and Pava Farkas' second child was Baylah (born 1892). She had four children. One died as a child, and two others died during the Holocaust. Baylah died around 1928. One daughter, Bruchelah, made it through the war and ended up living in Marseilles, France. She married Martin Roth, and they had a son named Simon. We often visited her and her family on trips to France. Simon made his living trading gold, which he initially did with his father. He often traveled to New York for business, and as a result we saw him frequently. Simon married and had two children.

Wolf and Pava's third child was Shlomo or Solomon (1895–1944). Solomon married Golda (Aranka) Marton, who was born one year after he was. Solomon was a farmer in Vilyatana. He had several animals and a nice amount of land. They had a son named Wolf Farkas, who was born on January 22, 1922. Wolf also survived the Holocaust and in fact, returned to live in the area, which was now under the rule of the Soviet Union. He lived there until the mid to late 1970s, when the Soviet Union made it easier for Jews to emigrate. Wolf and his family moved to Israel, and I will write more about that later.

The fourth child of Wolf and Pava Farkas, my grandfather, Samuel Farkas, was followed by Yita, who was born on December 26, 1903, and died during World War II. Yita's husband, Meilich Marton (born 1898) was a shoemaker. Yita had a twin sister Chaya (Hani), who died within a month of her birth. Yita had two children. One died during the Holocaust and the other, Hensha, survived. In the mid to late 1970s, she was also able to take advantage of the Soviet Union's relaxed emigration rules and eventually moved to Borough Park in Brooklyn.

The seventh child was Avrum, who was born on March 8, 1905. He, too, had a store in Vilyatana. He had either four or five children. The eighth child of Wolf and Pava was my maternal grandmother, Bruchela (Barbara), who was born on March 13, 1907. She married Efraim Davidovic, and they had three children— Esther, who was born on August 10, 1929; Regine, who was born on April 12, 1933; and Victor, who was born on December 11, 1941. Finally, the ninth child of Wolf and Pava Farkas was Moshe, who was born in 1913 and died in the Holocaust in 1943. Moshe was a roofer. He was the father of two sets of twins. Moshe died in the Theresienstadt concentration camp, and his wife and children also perished during the Holocaust (see Appendix B for Farkas Family Tree).

The Szobel (Sobel) Tree: Paternal Grandmother

My grandfather Samuel Farkas married Brana Szobel (Sobel) in 1921. Brana's parents were Hersh (Herman) Szobel, who was born on August 3, 1873, and Czili Szobel née Farkas, who was born in June of 1881. Hersh Szobel's parents were Moses Szobel and Rivka Szobel née Farkas, both of whom were from Vilyatana. Czili or Czina Szobel's parents were Zelman Farkas, who was from Vilyatana, and Brana Farkas née Motyovicz, who was from Danylovo, a small village 20 kilometers from Khust in Transcarpathia.

Hersh and Czili Szobel had at least five children. As far as I can tell from records on JewishGen.com, Brana, who was born on September 21, 1902, was the eldest. Zelman Szobel was born on July 1, 1904 and married Ethel Stern. They had six children. Hani Szobel was born on January 26, 1907. She married Michail Esner in Velky Berezny in 1930, which coincided with my paternal grandparents, Samuel and Brana Farkas, moving there. They probably were instrumental in arranging Hani's marriage at that time. Hani had four children. Brana's two youngest siblings were twin sisters born on October 17, 1909. One twin is recorded as Helena Szobel, the other as Farkas Szobel. However, there is a death record for Serena Szobel, who died at age 14 on November 21, 1923, and I believe this is the real name of the second twin (see Appendix C for Sobel Family Tree).*

---

*On the website *MyHeritage.com* I have a family tree that goes into greater detail regarding members of the Farkas, Sobel and Davidovic families.

The Davidovic Tree: Maternal Grandfather

My grandfather Efraim Davidovic, who lived from October 12, 1905, to May 12, 1970, married Bruchala (Barbara) Farkas (the eighth child of Wolf and Pava Farkas) on August 21, 1928. Efraim's parents were Jutko Davidovic and Pava Dina Davidovic née Saxze. Both were from Vilyatana. Unfortunately, they both died during the Spanish Flu pandemic of 1918–1920. Pava died on September 11, 1918, and Jutko died on June 6, 1920. Efraim was 15 at the time of his father's death and was subsequently taken in by an older sister, Malka.

Efraim had four brothers as well. I only knew one of them—Binyamin, who was born on April 1, 1908, and settled in Haifa after World War II. According to records, one brother, Abraham, died on February 20, 1916, at the age of 19. There was also a sister, who is listed as Mozes (Malia) and was born on July 1, 1911. Like Efraim, Binyamin and Mozes were also taken in by Malka. Efraim apprenticed with a shoemaker and learned how to make and repair shoes. At the age of 19, he was drafted and served in the Czechoslovakian Army and was based in the city of Olomouc. Meanwhile, being a shoemaker was not a good way to make much of a living because so many people were poor and could not afford to spend money on shoes (see Appendix D for Davidovic Family Tree).*

---

*Recorded names and spellings of names changed from decade to decade, depending on which government was in charge. In addition, families named children with Hebrew/Yiddish names (usually after a deceased relative), and when they had to, they provided the records office with a secular name, which often changed. For example, Pava could be Pava on one record and Tova on another record. Also, one could find one first name on a state birth certificate and another on a marriage or death certificate. Birthdates could also be incorrect because they would remember someone was born on Yom Kippur or three days before Purim. This was obviously an imprecise way to keep records.

2

MY MOTHER'S FAMILY LEAVES VILYATANA

ACCORDING TO MY PATERNAL GRANDFATHER, Samuel Farkas, his mother, Pava Farkas (her husband had already passed away), arranged the marriage between his younger sister, Bruchela, and Efraim Davidovic. Efraim's sister, Malka, who had taken in her three youngest siblings when their parents died during the Spanish Flu epidemic, also helped put the marriage together. The Davidovic family, although poor, was "sehr ehrlich" (very honorable). After marrying, Efraim and Bruchela had a small one-story house with some land. They raised several animals, including chickens and a goat. There may have been other animals, but my mother always mentioned the eggs from the chickens and the warm milk they drank from the goat.

Efraim and Bruchela's first child was my mother, Esther. She was born on August 10, 1929. Her sister, Regine (Rivka), was born April 12, 1933. My mother remembered Vilyatana as a pretty place with a great deal of room to run around outside. There were family and friends around all the time. Living next door to them was Aunt Malka. They would walk to their grandmother's (Pava Farkas) store by themselves to get "*tzicherlich*" (candies). They didn't have much, but it was a place my mother and Aunt Regine remember fondly. She described Jewish holidays there as "wonderful." They had big seders on Passover with a lot of people in attendance. They built a *sukkah*, where they ate on Sukkot. She remembers getting and giving "*shalach monas*" on Purim, which was fun because they had a big family and many friends with whom to exchange these gifts of food and drink.

Belgium

Due to the fact there was not a lot of money to be made as a shoemaker, my maternal grandfather, Efraim, inquired about other opportunities and found out Belgium was recruiting workers for their coal and steel industries. He applied for a job and started working in a coal mine on March 11, 1930, in La Louviere in the Walloon area of Belgium. He worked above ground and sent money back to his family. He went back to Vilyatana two years later, on July 8, 1932, for several months so that he could be with his family. He then returned to Belgium at the beginning of 1933 and settled in Liege. The plan was for him to make some more money working in the coal mines and then again return to Vilyatana, but the political landscape in Europe started to change around that time. As a result, in the years that followed, he began to feel that his family might be safer in Belgium than in Vilyatana because Belgium had declared neutrality in 1936 and Hungary was about to annex the area of Transcarpathia. Hungary had also come to rely heavily on trade with Nazi Germany and Italy. In addition, there was a rising nationalistic movement in Hungary (in 1940 it would become the fourth country to join the Axis powers).

In the summer of 1938, my grandmother Bruchela, along with my mother, Esther, who was 8 years old at the time, and her sister, Regine, who was 4, left Vilyatana for Belgium to be with my grandfather. They joined him in Liege, which was urban and thus far different from Vilyatana. My grandmother's family was opposed to the move because Belgium was considered "a *tref land*" (unkosher). In Liege, Efraim, Bruchela, my mother and Regine lived on the second or third floor of a building, which was far different from their little house in Vilyatana. There is a story I often heard in which my aunt Regine, trying to understand the family's new circumstances, asked, "How will the poor people know where we are?" She had always given a *krona* (a coin) to beggars who came to their door in Vilyatana.

Nevertheless, my mother's family adjusted to Liege, made friends and also established relationships with more distant family members who lived there. Esther and Regine went to school, and Efraim worked in the coal mines, while Bruchela took care of the children and their home. By this time, my grandfather was working underground at the mines on the night-shift safety team. Esther and Regine later described their early childhood in Liege as fairly normal. They had friends, went to school and enjoyed time with their parents. Their first address in Liege was 16 rue Large.

Belgium was and continues to be a country divided linguistically. It is French-speaking in the south and east, and Flemish-speaking in the north and west. About 8 million people lived in Belgium before World War II, and most of them were Catholic. There were 70,000—75,000 Jews living there, mostly in the cities of Antwerp, Brussels, Charleroi and Liege. The majority of them were recent immigrants from Germany and Eastern Europe, people like my grandparents. Thus, only a small minority of the Jewish population were Belgian citizens.

Despite Belgium's declaration of neutrality, the German army entered the country on May 10, 1940. Shortly thereafter, the country was put under German military rule. In October of 1940, the German military administration adopted a series of anti-Jewish laws. Jews were henceforth required to register with their local municipalities and list their monetary and economic assets (homes, stores, etc.). Jewish shops and businesses had to have a sign in the window indicating Jewish ownership. Soon the businesses were transferred to German ownership in a process referred to as "Aryanization."

Even so, life was somewhat normal during the latter part of 1940. However, as World War II intensified, money, food and other necessities became less and less available. My mother recalled how she once ate a piece of bread and her mother became angry, saying, "Now your father won't have enough to eat." But my grandfather told her it was O.K. because a growing child needed to eat as well.

Meanwhile, by 1941 restrictive laws against Jews increased, and my mother and Aunt Regine were no longer allowed to attend school. They had to adjust to the fact that they were basically homebound. Jews were also required to wear a yellow Star of David on their clothing to identify them as Jewish. My mother would be sent out on quick errands to get milk or bread, as it was dangerous to be out too long, especially while wearing the yellow star. Having a star on your clothing was an open invitation to being harassed, and it also resulted in being shunned by friends and neighbors.

When my mother was sent on an errand, sometimes she would take the risk of not wearing the yellow star. One time, she saw a German soldier turning toward her on her way back from an errand and she averted eye contact and froze. She didn't know what to do and stood silently for what felt like a long time to her. She looked up and saw him motioning to her with his rifle to get going. She made it home and started to cry. Clearly, everyone was scared. Jews were being targeted, and people frequently disappeared overnight. To further complicate matters, on December 11, 1941, Victor Davidovic was born. My mother now had a little brother. My grandmother stayed in the hospital overnight at the Hospital de Baviere. Everyone was happy—or at least as happy as they could be under the circumstances—and the *bris* was held in secret, with only immediate family members and a few other people present. Esther was then 12 and Regine 8, and the world in which they lived was becoming increasingly perilous.

My mother used to tell me how her friends were surprised that she was Jewish when she started wearing the Star of David on her coat. Around that time, Jews were summoned to work in the local munitions factory. My mother remembers young people were gathered and told to bring some clothing with them to go to work but that they never came back. One time, my grandmother was summoned and she went to the German Military Command with her three children and told the officer that she, herself, would go to work if he was willing to watch her two girls and the baby. He looked at her aghast and luckily told her to go home. My grandmother, as I knew her, was quiet and rarely spoke to us beyond asking if we were hungry or needed anything. To think of her with that kind of chutzpah is kind of shocking but makes me proud.

Finding Refuge in a Convent-Orphanage (1942–1945)

In 1942, the Jews in Belgium began to be deported, with the deportations varying by city. In Antwerp, 67 percent of the Jews were deported. In Liege, however, the figure was 35 percent, the lowest number in any of the areas where there was a significant number of Jews. The primary destination of these deportations was Auschwitz, the Nazi concentration camp in Poland. These deportations usually occurred during the night, when people were sleeping. The German soldiers would show up at an apartment without warning, forcefully gather everyone together and then put them in trucks, never to be seen again. My mother remembers it being quiet at night and then hearing the German soldiers, in their boots, coming up the street, a sound that made all Jews terrified that they and their family would be next. My grandparents realized the situation in Liege was becoming more intolerable and it wouldn't be too long before the Germans came for them. They spoke to their rabbi to see what they could do, knowing the Committee for the Defense of Jews (CDJ) was helping to hide children with the help of private citizens and elements of the Catholic Church. The rabbi himself had two sons hidden separately with two families. Furthermore, the CDJ, while they kept records of all those who were hidden, would not tell the parents where the children were hidden for obvious safety reasons.

My grandparents' landlady, Madame Van Sprang, was a widow and a practicing Catholic. She was able to arrange with the priest of her parish (Saint-Pholien) to get my mother and her two siblings into the St. Augustine convent/orphanage in the village of Gellik, in the Flemish-speaking part of Belgium, about 25 miles from Liege.

It is a village in the city of Lanaken, in the province of Limbourg. All three children were given identification papers and false names. They all took on the surname Jansen, which was a common Flemish name. Regine and Victor were common Catholic names, so they kept their given names and became Regine Jansen and Victor Jansen. My mother could not keep the name Esther, as it was instantly recognizable as a Jewish name, so she became Maria Jansen. There was also an agreement that, if my grandparents did not survive the war, Madame Van Sprang would adopt Victor, who was then 8 months old. Esther and Regine would become Catholics (baptized) and stay in the convent. My grandparents agreed to this arrangement in order to save their children. Esther, being the oldest, was told by her parents to look after and take care of her siblings and to remember she was a "*Yiddisha tochter*" (a Jewish daughter). This was not unlike what her grandmother had told her mother when they left Vilyatana to move to Belgium. The decision to give up her children, especially her 8-month-old son, who was still being nursed, haunted my grandmother the rest of her life. And my mother noted how terrifying it was to be away from her parents and to have the responsibility of taking care of her sister and baby brother.

The three children arrived in Saint Augustine ("Sint-Augustine" in Dutch) in the middle of August 1942. The convent had been founded in 1901 and was led by the Sisters of St. Joseph; the orphanage had been added in 1905. (The convent closed in 1980, and the remaining nuns took up residence in a retirement home in Lanaken. The building went through some renovations and is now a music school.)

Overnight, the lives of my mother and her sister and brother changed dramatically. They were separated from their parents with no idea if or when they would ever be reunited. They now had different names and had to learn a different language (Flemish), as well as all the Catholic rituals that the Catholic children had been following for years. My mother and Regine had to learn the basics of the Catholic mass in a few hours. The priest had to teach them how to kneel, bow their heads and make the sign of the cross when praying. They had to hide their true identities and adopt new personas. My mother told the story of how she had to remember to respond to her new name, Maria, when someone addressed her. Remembering her name was not that easy for a while. In the beginning, at times, she hesitated when someone called her "Maria," and at one point, another girl asked her, *"Du bist ein Jude?"* (Are you a Jew?) My mother immediately became scared and turned red, fearing they had been found out. And then, the girl told her, *"Ich bin ein Jude auch"* (I am a Jew, too). Her name was Rita (which was her real name), and they became best friends for the remainder of their time in the convent. Rita also had a younger sister in the convent. My mother lost touch with Rita after the war, but they later reunited in Israel in 1979.

My mother said that, while she was in the convent, it seemed there was praying all the time. They also had to receive communion and go to confession. She often related that she didn't know what to confess, as she hadn't done anything wrong. She would confess to lying, as she was lying that she was Maria Jansen and Catholic.

She and Regine went to classes in catechism and mathematics and learned vocational skills, such as sewing. They had chores as well. Esther volunteered to work in the nursery and was eventually assigned there, and that allowed her to look after Victor and frequently feed him. However, she said she was often worried about being found out and that, if her real identity was discovered, her sister and brother would be in peril as well. She also worried whether she would ever see her parents again. This was a lot for a 13-year-old to deal with. She also knew that Regine was relying on her, so she had to put up a brave front for her sister.

Esther and Regine slept on cots that were in a large upstairs hall where dozens of other children also slept. Before they went to bed, they had to get on their knees and pray. Once they were in bed, they were not allowed to leave it until morning. Regine often had to go to the bathroom at night due to a weak bladder but was afraid of getting caught, so Esther would go with her. If they were spotted, they had to kneel by their bed the rest of the night. Regine does not remember many details of this time in her life, but she still talks about kneeling by the bed for hours.

My mother described her fear of being exposed as a Jew because she had no idea how many of the nuns or priests knew which of the children were Jewish, or how many of them were committed to keeping the children's real identities concealed. As far as my mother knew, only the local parish priest and the Mother Superior at the convent knew about their true identities as Jews, although it seems clear that other nuns knew as well. For instance, my mother worried about Victor because he was circumcised, and that was one way that German soldiers would check a boy's identity. But at least some of the nuns had the same concern because, when they learned that German soldiers might be coming, they would hide Victor and other Jewish boys until the soldiers left.

Fortunately, Madame Van Sprang and the local parish priest who arranged for them to come to the convent/orphanage visited periodically. This enabled my grandparents to know how their children were doing and for Esther and Regine to learn how their mother and father were faring. And through it all, my mother was told to never admit she was Jewish.

My mother also had her first menstrual cycle while in the convent. She had no idea what was happening to her and said she thought she was dying because of all the blood. She didn't tell anyone and hid the underwear under her bed. One of the nuns found the hidden clothes and summoned her. The nun then told her, "Now you are a woman!" There was no other explanation offered to my mother, who was 13 at the time.

There were also bombings in the area throughout their stay in the convent. The sirens would go off, and the children would go into the cellar for safety. Esther was told by the Mother Superior to take Victor with her and make sure to hide with him, so any German soldiers who showed up would not see him. During one of the bombings, they were in the cellar for almost two weeks. When the church bells tolled, it was a signal for the children to come back out of the cellar. She said it was sometimes horrible when she looked outside, for it resembled a battlefield, with dead bodies on the ground.

During this time, my grandparents often stayed with a Catholic family they knew from Vilyatana. The family lived in a somewhat rural area outside of Liege. It seemed safer than being in Liege. At times, they would come back to their apartment on rue Large, in Liege, but only for a short time. One time, my grandmother was desperate to see her children as she hadn't heard anything for quite a while. Despite the risk involved, she went on the train to Gellik in an attempt to see them. On the way there, at one of the stations, German soldiers boarded the train and began asking everyone to show their papers. When she observed what was going on, she jumped off the train. She luckily escaped but ended up injuring herself and bleeding from her head. Although she failed to get to Gellik, it was another example of her bravery and determination.

My mother, and her sister and brother, were adequately fed and clothed during their stay in the convent, but as the war went on provisions became scarcer. Still, my mother always felt she was lucky despite the fear that she might never see her parents again and despite the burdens she faced in looking out for her siblings. Dealing with all of that, she said, was very, very hard. She used to say how she was a good Catholic while she was at the convent, and when she was visited by Madame Van Sprang and was given updates about her parents, she would feel God had answered her prayers as a Catholic. Then she would remember her mother's words about being a Jewish daughter. Amid the constant fear, this would leave her feeling confused and guilty. That fear and guilt were ever present.

Liege was liberated by the Allied forces on September 8, 1944. My mother remembers how they were waiting at the convent for their parents to come and take them back home, for the family to finally be reunited. And several days after the liberation, the reunion took place, with Esther, Regine and Victor being picked up by their mother and father. They had managed to evade the Germans by moving around and staying with various non-Jewish friends from Vilyatana. In the aftermath of the liberation, they had also vacated their apartment on rue Large and moved into a small, two-floor walk-up apartment at 13 rue Mathieu Polain.

Meanwhile, World War II had not ended. In fact, between November 1944 and January 1945 the Germans were launching V1 and V2 rockets towards London with a failure rate of 10 to 20 percent. Some of the misfiring rockets landed and exploded in Belgium and France. One instance occurred on Sunday, December 17, 1944, while my grandfather (Efraim) was taking Esther and Regine to a flea market near the Meuse River (*la Meuse*). It was a beautiful sunlit day, and as they were about to return home, a German rocket exploded on their block. They could actually see the explosion from the flea market. They ran home to see if my grandmother and Victor, now 3 years old, were safe. Luckily, while most of the block was damaged and 10 people were killed and many more injured, the houses facing rue Mathieu Polain had limited damage. The plaster from the ceiling in their apartment had fallen, but neither Victor nor my grandmother was injured. Still, this incident was enough for my grandparents to decide to again place the three children back in the convent, where they would be safer. They stayed there until May 1945, when the war in Europe ended and it was safe for the family to again be together.

Coming back home to their parents was not a simple matter, as Esther and Regine wanted to continue to go to church to pray. Their mother was very upset about this, but their father instinctively knew to let them continue to go to church in order to ease the transition back to their previous life. After several months, they no longer needed to go. My mother said that the priest at the local church made her feel uncomfortable, and if she didn't go to church, Regine wouldn't go, either. As for little Victor, he had no idea who his parents were and frequently cried out for Sister Lasca from the convent. He did not sleep well, he cried a lot and he was often inconsolable. This was very painful for my grandmother, but eventually Victor adjusted to being back home.

But while the war was over, the situation they were living in was difficult. Belgium's economy, not surprisingly, was in bad shape. The neighborhood they lived in was filled with rubble caused by the rockets that had landed there. Even their apartment, which had no closets, was a reminder of how disorienting things had become. My mother recalls putting all of her things on a sheet on the floor.

At this point, my mother was almost 16 and did not want to return to school. She said that, while she was at the convent, her life had been consumed by prayers, school, chores, volunteering in the nursery to take care of Victor and watching out for Regine. She wanted a change. My grandfather said she had to do something to earn money if she did not go to school. So, she decided to take sewing classes to become a seamstress and did this for the next few years. She also joined the Jewish youth group in the local synagogue and met others her age. Regine, meanwhile, continued with her schooling as she was still only 12 years old. Efraim, my grandfather, went back to working on the safety team in the coal mines, and he also repaired shoes on the side. Victor, not yet 4 years old, stayed at home with my grandmother.

My mother and her sister and brother had been robbed of normal childhoods. They had been separated from their parents and then lived in constant fear of being "found out" or being betrayed by others. Other hidden children were less fortunate because they ended up losing their parents for good. But because these children weren't deported to labor or death camps, the challenges they went through were not deemed worthy of much attention, and it wasn't until many years later that they were. Some of that recognition came in May 1991, when the first International Gathering of Children Hidden during World War II took place—in New York City. In all, one and a half million Jewish children were exterminated by the Nazis, and about 100,000 survived, including my mother and her two siblings and many others who had been hidden. It is to their everlasting credit that so many of them went on to become caring and resourceful adults.

3

MY FATHER'S FAMILY LEAVES VILYATANA

MY PATERNAL GRANDFATHER, SAMUEL, was a very bright student, so he was sent to study in a yeshiva near Szatmar when he was in his early teens. Like his father, Wolf (*Smila*) Farkas, he also learned how to be a lumberman. He told me he could go into a forest or simply a wooded area and quickly calculate how much lumber he could accumulate in a day, the order in which trees should be cut down, what kind of monetary yield he could get and how long it would take. He determined which trees would be used for firewood, telephone poles, railroad ties and even pencils to be shipped to Germany. He was able to lease the land with the proviso that he would replant trees after the work was done. In effect, he was a contractor, and he would hire hundreds of workers to do the various jobs necessary to get the trees converted into lumber and then sent either down the river or put on wagons so that the wood would reach the intended buyers.

Even though he had been an Orthodox yeshiva student, he carried a gun and was highly respected in the town and at work.

My grandfather and my paternal grandmother, Brana, were married in 1921, when he was 23. While in Vilyatana, Brana Farkas gave birth to their first child, Regina (*Rivka*), who was born on December 28, 1921. Sara (*Serena*) was born on April 1, 1924. Their third child was my father, Wilhelm (*Wolf*). He was born on September 18, 1926, although he entered a different date of birth (October 27, 1929) when he entered the ghetto during World War ll and then Auschwitz. As a result, many documents from the war list the altered date as his birthday. Why a different birth date? It may have been because Willy and Moishe, his younger brother, tried not to be separated during the Holocaust. Moishe (*Moritz*) was born on February 20, 1929, according to records from JewishGen, or February 25, 1929, as noted on all other documents completed by Moishe. Either way, my father's decision to alter his birth date put their ages much closer together.

Meanwhile, sometime between the actual birth of my father and the birth of my uncle Moishe, the family moved to a bigger town called Berezna, in Yiddish, and often called Velky Berezny by Czechs or Nagy Berezny by native Hungarians. Since my father was a toddler when the move from Vilyatana took place, he did not remember much about it.

Velky Berezny was in the Ung district of Transcarpathia. It was north of Vilyatana and 21 miles north-northeast of the city of Uzhhorod. Velky Berezny had a *gymnasium*, or high school, that included students from the surrounding villages. The nearest hospital was in Uzhhorod. The town had four doctors, three lawyers and other professionals. It also had a bank, a few small factories, a distillery and over 40 other businesses. There were cars for the doctors to make house calls and one ambulance to drive to the hospital in Uzhhorod in case of an emergency. Velky Berezny became the regional center of the smaller surrounding villages. By 1941, Jews were the majority of the estimated population of 3,000 inhabitants. The rest were Rusyns and Gypsies.

As was previously noted, Moishe was born in Velky Berezny in February 1929. Samuel and Brana's fifth child, Deena, was born on October 7, 1930, followed by Bentzion on June 16, 1936, and Chaim on October 15, 1938. My grandmother's sister, Hani, married Michail Esner from Velky Berezny and settled there as well. They had at least four children born between 1930 and 1938. As a result, there were close relationships between the two families.

My father and his siblings went to public school in the morning and to *cheder*, or religious school, in the afternoon. My uncle Moishe used to say how the teachers in the public school were anti-Semitic, in part because some Jews had joined the Hungarian army, which engaged in conflict with the Ukrainians. As a result, anti-Semitism was present in the Transcarpathian area, which was heavily Jewish. Indeed, my father often said after the war that "the Ukrainians were worse" than the Germans.

Samuel and Brana and their children lived in a house that my father described as beautiful. He often mentioned that the house had a colored window in the front and that it was a nice-sized property with a garden. Samuel had done well working as a lumberman and forester and he was often hired by the government of Czechoslovakia to manage various projects, as they knew he was knowledgeable and trusted his judgment. He put a store in the front of the house where Brana could sell sugar, tobacco, onions and other items. This way, she would have access to money when he was away working in the Carpathian Mountains. They also had two cows, chickens and geese. My grandfather told me that before he headed to work in the mountains, my grandmother would make him some sandwiches and pack a rucksack for him, and that he carried another bag with his *tallis*, *tefillin* and *siddur*, or prayer book. It was important that he pray every morning. He also carried a rifle.

At Elissa's bat mitzvah in 1994, an elderly gentleman introduced himself to me and asked what my father's name was. I told him it was Wilhelm. He asked if he came from Berezna (Velky Berezny) before the war. When I confirmed he had lived in Berezna, he told me that his family and my dad's had been backyard neighbors. After the service, I introduced my father and my uncle Moishe to this gentleman, whose name was Zoltan Spiegel. He was elated, as was my father, to see someone from the old country after 50 years. They reminisced, and my father went on to become friendly with Zoltan, as did I. He shared stories about Berezna and told me he was one of five children of an Orthodox Jewish family. Zoltan was also 14 years older than my father. His own father had been in the beer and liquor business and done very well for himself. Zoltan went to technical schools in the area and opened a radio and electrical supply shop in 1936. After the occupation of Czechoslovakia by Germany in 1939, Germany ceded the area to Hungary, which imposed restrictive laws on Jews. Zoltan and his father lost their licenses to operate their businesses. I can recall when my father told him how he and Moishe used to steal apples from the trees on the Spiegel family property. My father also marveled how the Spiegels had radios and other kinds of electric equipment. In the 1930s, this was considered rich and very modern.

I also heard stories from Zoltan of how my grandfather, Samuel Farkas, was very talented as a wordsmith and poet. During Purim, the townsfolk would gather to hear his festive Purim Spiel, which was written in rhyme in Yiddish. He would have lines in the poem about the various people in the town and the *shul*. Maybe it is Samuel from whom Elissa, my daughter, gets her poetic and story-telling talents.

Hungary Annexes the Area

The Transcarpathian territory became part of Czechoslovakia through the Treaty of Trianon on June 4, 1920. The region had a strong and vibrant Jewish presence, as the area had a long history of ethnic, religious and cultural diversity, and the various groups, including Jews, were able to more or less co-exist until the Hungarian occupation of 1938. In November of that year, the area was re-annexed by Hungary as part of the First Vienna Award, a treaty that was an outgrowth of the infamous Munich Agreement with Nazi Germany, which resulted in the partitioning of Czechoslovakia. Many older Jews in Transcarpathia welcomed the news of the return to Hungarian rule because they remembered the days of Emperor Franz Joseph and a society in which egalitarianism generally prevailed. However, it wasn't long before the new authorities decreed the expulsion of all Jews without Hungarian citizenship. There was already a good deal of Rusyn and Ukrainian nationalism, with anti-Semitic undertones. Now, the Hungarians were sharing a supremacist agenda with the Rusyns and Ukrainians, who were newly committed to ridding the area of Jews and other "undesirables." As a result, Polish and Russian Jews who were long-term residents of Transcarpathia (many for over 50 years), as well as Jews from Western Europe who were in the region, were deported over the border into Ukraine and, as World War II took hold, turned over to the German Einsatzgruppe commando. Einsatzgruppen were Schutzstaffel (SS) paramilitary death squads or "mobile killing units" who became best known for the systematic murder of Jews in Soviet territories.

Many Jews lost their businesses and livelihoods. The education became Magyarized (Hungarian-dominated), to the detriment of Jewish students. Jews were openly harassed in the streets, often by people they knew. And the brutality of the Hungarian police surprised many Jews. On November 20, 1940, Hungary signed the Tripartite Pact and entered the war on Germany's side. A series of anti-Jewish laws were enacted, depriving Jews of civil rights. Among other things, Jews were not allowed to have telephones or radios. Later, Jews were not allowed to attend school. They couldn't walk on sidewalks and instead had to walk in the gutter.

On August 27 and 28 of 1941, thousands of Jews and other "undesirables" were marched 16 kilometers and told to undress. It is estimated over 23,600 in all were then machine-gunned to death in Kamenets Podolski, which is in western Ukraine. It is estimated that 14,000 to 16,000 of the victims were Hungarian Jews. It was the first large massacre of World War II. The perpetrators included the Einsatzgruppen, Hungarian soldiers and the Ukrainian auxiliary police, as well as other local police groups. Many eyewitnesses stated that those who carried out the massacre made no effort to hide their deeds from the local population. We know of six Jewish families without Hungarian citizenship in Vilyatana and several families from Velky Berezny who were massacred in this incident.

Amid all this horror, my grandfather was fortunate the Hungarian government still needed his expertise. They assigned him to work in the forest, but now he was on salary. Rivka, his eldest daughter, was his bookkeeper, and my father and some of his cousins from Vilyatana sometimes worked with them as well. Meanwhile, by 1942, most Jews in Europe lived in abject poverty, with their businesses confiscated, and many young adult males were forced into labor camps. It became increasingly difficult to simply stay alive. Those who remained had to live off whatever savings they may have had. Nevertheless, despite the many dangers to Jews in Transcarpathia, the situation was worse in many other parts of Europe. The Jews in Transcarpathia heard about the atrocities and mass murders from the influx of Jewish refugees from Poland. Many local Jews found it hard to believe these stories. "We thought they were exaggerated," survivors would recall years later, even though more and more refugees were relating the same story.

4

FROM GHETTO TO DEATH CAMPS

Uzhhorod Ghetto

In March 1944, German units invaded Hungary and took control of the entire region. They looted, smashed and closed down the Jewish shops that still remained. All Jews were confined to their homes, except at specified hours. They had to wear a round yellow patch on their clothing. This was later replaced by the yellow Star of David. The fate of the Jews in Transcarpathia was soon transferred into the hands of Adolf Eichmann and the SS. On April 12, 1944, the order to isolate the Jews of Transcarpathia in ghettos was issued. Seventeen ghettos were set up, and Jews were rounded up, forced to leave their homes and placed in these confined, impoverished areas. Families were told to take only a few items—two sets of clothing, food and bedding material—when they moved to one of these enclosures. They were also told to lock their homes or apartments and put the keys in an envelope on which they were to write their old address. They gave the envelope to the Judenrat, the Jewish Council established by the Germans. Of course, they never saw their homes again as they were plundered and looted the day they were forced out of them. At this point, there were no Jews left in either Velky Berezny or Vilyatana. They had all been rounded up and forced into the ghettos.

On April 17, 1944, my father's family, including his mother and six of his seven siblings, were told to move into one of the ghettos. They were placed in the improvised Moskovitz Brickyard ghetto in Uzhhorod, which was about 20 miles southwest of Velky Berezny. Uzhhorod, its Ukrainian name, was also known as Ungvar (the Hungarian name). The name is derived from the Uzh River and the surrounding county, which was called Ung by the Hungarians. In addition to the Moskovitz Brickyard ghetto, another one was created at the Gluck Lumberyard. Families went from being in a warm, comfortable home to living in a 10-by-10-foot room in a cold, barren factory with a tiny fraction of their belongings.

My father was 17 at the time, and my uncle Moishe was 14. My father talked about how, as the oldest son, he had to find work and look for scraps of food for the family. If he could find a cigarette or a cigarette butt, he could trade it for food. He talked about finding potato peels so they could be put in the family's soup. He also worked whenever it was possible to do so. Getting out of the ghetto for the part of the day when he was working meant there was a possibility of finding things he could bring back to the family—either items to use immediately or to trade for something else.

Meanwhile, his father and his eldest sister, Rivka, were on a job for the government in the Carpathian Mountains when the rest of the family were expelled from their home and brought to the ghetto. At the time, my grandfather also had one of his brothers, Shlomo, working with him and at least one of his nephews—Shlomo's son, Wolf. When my grandfather found out that his family had been taken from its home and sent to the brickyard, he and Rivka immediately went there to be with everyone else. After my grandfather arrived, he and my father, along with my uncle Moishe, would volunteer for work. My grandfather noted how Moishe was tall for his age and looked older than 14. And my father became increasingly adept in trading what he found or was given outside the ghetto. Sometimes that meant obtaining bread or potatoes for the family.

The entire family of nine (or 10, as Rivka had married Bela Deutsch) was crowded into that 10-foot-by-10-foot space. The conditions were cruel and unsanitary. Food was in short supply, and medical services were non-existent. Serious diseases like typhus broke out. Jews, especially Orthodox Jews with beards, were humiliated, brutalized and beaten by the German soldiers who were stationed in Transcarpathia, and by their Hungarian supporters. It was not uncommon to pass by Jews who had been beaten to death, their bodies left in the street. Thus, when my father's family and other Jews in the ghettos were told of upcoming deportations, they thought wherever they would be sent would surely be better than what they were already enduring.

Deportations: May 1944–July 1945

Starting on May 15, 1944, over 14,000 Jews a day were taken from the Transcarpathia ghettos to Auschwitz until the last deportation on June 6, 1944. From the two Uzhhorod ghettos—the brickyard and the lumberyard—there were five trains, or cattle cars, that deported the Jews to Auschwitz from May 17 to May 31, 1944. Those from these two ghettos were forced onto the cattle cars under a hail of physical and mental abuse. They had to undress and were forced to watch as the Gestapo and others working on behalf of the Nazis tore their clothes to see if something had been sewn into them. Only then were the clothes returned. At the same time, the Jews' identification cards were torn up, making them "unpersons." In all, there were between 90 and 100 people in each enclosed car, with one bucket of water for the two-to-three-day journey. There was also one bucket to use as a toilet, with no windows or fresh air and space to lie down. The stench of vomit, urine and excrement, and the lack of air, food and water, resulted in many people dying in the cattle cars from starvation, dehydration and suffocation. Some committed suicide and others lost their minds.

My father and his family were on the fourth train, which left Uzhhorod on May 27 and arrived at Auschwitz on May 28, which was during Shavuot. On these five trains from the two Uzhhorod ghettos, 16,168 people were deported to Auschwitz. About 70 percent—11,319—were killed immediately upon arrival.

On the fourth train (train number 49), which included my father's immediate family of nine, 2,988 Jews arrived at Auschwitz. Only 211 men and 232 women from that group were selected for work camps. The rest, about 85 percent, were killed by gassing upon arrival, including my grandmother (Brana Farkas) and the three youngest siblings (Deena, Ben Zion and Chaim). The Germans did not separate mothers from the children, calculating that the children would go quietly into the gas showers with their mothers, all of them thinking they were going to be deloused. The last train from Uzhorod left on May 31, 1944. At that point, the city was declared "*Judenrein*"—free of Jews.

Auschwitz and Other Concentration Camps

Auschwitz consisted of dozens of concentration and extermination camps. It had been built by the Germans and was run by the SS. The main camps were Auschwitz I (originally for Polish prisoners of war), Auschwitz II-Birkenau and Auschwitz III-Monowitz. At first, the trains arrived near a railroad station, and the Jews who staggered off them then had to walk to the camp, passing through the iron gates with the infamous phrase *Arbeit Macht Frei* (Work makes one free) and into the camp itself. Between May and July 1944, the cattle cars stopped by the area around the crematoria, which is where the train with my father's family and other relatives ended up. Once the cattle cars arrived there, all the Jews were ordered to get out and line up and to move quickly towards the SS officers and doctors for the selection process. They were greeted by vicious barking dogs and a special squad called the Sunder Kommando, made up of Jews and Soviet POWs, who removed the corpses from the cars and any goods the Jews had brought with them on the awful journey.

When my father's family arrived at Auschwitz, the men were separated from the women and children. My father, who was 17, and my grandfather, Samuel, went on the left line. My grandmother (Brana), Rivka (age 23), Sara (20), Uncle Moishe (14), Deena (12), Ben Zion (8) and Chaim (6) went on the other line. My father then pulled Uncle Moishe to go with him and my grandfather. The lines proceeded towards the SS officers and doctors. My father, Moishe and my grandfather were deemed fit to work and they were registered and later given a number. My father and Moishe were then led to a place to undress, and had their heads shaved. They were also disinfected before showering. Their clothes were taken, and they were given striped prison uniforms and a hat. They were registered and on May 31, 1944, they each had their assigned number tattooed on their left arm, with Moishe branded with *A-11029* and my father with *A-11030*. Jewish prisoners were no longer called by their names, only by their number. This was all part of the dehumanization process. "You were never the same again," Moishe stated in his Shoah interview many years later.

Rivka and Sara, the two oldest daughters, were deemed fit for work and more than likely experienced the same process as my father and Moishe. My grandmother and the three youngest children were selected for the gas chamber. Their line looked like the other lines, and they were taken to a room to undress, supposedly to be deloused and disinfected before showering. However, they were led to a large room that had a sign saying *"Bade"* (shower), but instead of water, Zyklon B gas was emitted from the shower heads and within 10 minutes everyone in the room was dead. Auschwitz had four gas chambers, which could hold up to 2,000 victims at a time. According to witnesses, family members died hugging one another, with mothers sometimes frozen in a seated position on the ground, embracing their children. Afterwards, the bodies were burned in the crematoria. During this period of the Hungarian deportations, from May to July 1944, the Auschwitz gas chambers were working at maximum capacity, killing 12,000 Jews per day. I can recall my father always saying Kaddish for his mother and three younger siblings on the second night of Shavuot. And if my father had not pulled Uncle Moishe off the line with their mother and onto his line, Moishe probably would have died in the gas chambers as well.

My grandfather was with his two sons in Auschwitz for a few days and then was sent to Buchenwald, in Germany, and several other labor camps (*arbeitslager*). Meanwhile, my father and Uncle Moishe, both of them just teenagers, stayed together throughout their time in the concentration camps. They worked in several of the sub camps of Auschwitz, including Auschwitz-Birkenau (*Laurahutte*) in southern Poland, where they helped manufacture anti-tank and anti-aircraft artillery. Auschwitz-Monowitz, also known as Monowitz-Buna, was the labor camp in which they spent the longest time. They were there for between four and five months, according to my father. It was a plant that manufactured synthetic rubber for the German war effort. It was also the first concentration camp financed and built by private industry. The Nazis provided the cheap slave labor to the Buna Company, which operated the camp, which held 12,000 prisoners. It was a subsidiary of IG-Farben, the largest company in Europe at that time. IG-Farben supplied chemicals and pharmaceuticals to the Nazi war effort, including the Zyklon B gas that exterminated well over a million Jews in the gas chambers. My father said he mostly cleaned and packaged bolts and nuts while at Auschwitz-Monowitz. He also worked in the kitchen at times, which enabled him to eat better and to bring some food to the barracks for his brother and friends as well as to use for barter.

The life expectancy of the Jewish workers in Auschwitz-Monowitz was three to four months. For those who worked outside in the nearby mines, the life expectancy was one month. The conditions and daily life in the camps were barbaric, and when workers inevitably grew weak, the Nazis simply murdered them.

My father and Moishe were also in the Kattowitz (*Katowice*) sub-camp of Auschwitz-Birkenau, which was located north of Auschwitz (about an hour drive by car). I do not know what they did in that labor camp, but production of coal was a big part of the war effort in that region and town. They were there several months as well. The three labor camps—Laurahutte, Monowitz and Katowitz—were all part of the Auschwitz and Auschwitz-Birkenau concentration camp complex. Willy and Moishe also sometimes worked as masons in the labor camps and in Laurahutte; they also worked in the airplane parts factory.

The typical day in the Auschwitz labor camps often began at 4:30 a.m., an hour later in the winter. The block supervisor sounded a gong to wake them. Prisoners then had to wash and use the latrines quickly. If the guards felt they weren't doing it quickly enough, they would beat them and rush them out. The sanitary conditions themselves were atrocious, with only a few latrines and a lack of clean water for hundreds of prisoners. Each prisoner received a half liter of coffee substitute or tea in the morning, but no food. A second gong signaled roll call. The prisoners were lined up outside in rows of ten to be counted. They then had to wait for the SS officer's arrival for the counting to begin. In the winter, it was freezing, but it didn't matter. How long the prisoners waited outside to be counted depended upon the mood of the officer and whether there were escapees or other events that resulted in additional brutality toward the prisoners. In some instances, the guards could make the prisoners squat or stand with their hands raised above their heads for lengthy periods of time.

After roll call, the prisoners walked five abreast and went to their assigned place of work to begin the workday, which lasted from 10 to 11 hours. They were often forced to sing going to and coming from work. For lunch, the prisoners were given watery soup. Sometimes the soup had potatoes in it. Many described the soup as tasting foul or rancid. The evening meal consisted of 300 grams of bread that was frequently moldy, with a tablespoon of marmalade or margarine. Many prisoners saved some of the bread for the next morning.

A second roll call, like the morning roll call, occurred at 7:00 p.m. If a prisoner was missing, everyone would be forced to remain standing until the prisoner was found or the reason for his absence discovered. Sometimes, this took hours. There were also beatings to try to elicit information from the prisoners, and prisoners would even be hanged by the Germans as other prisoners were forced to watch. The prisoners were then marched back to the barracks. At 9:00 p.m., the lights were extinguished. The prisoners slept on either wooden pallets or cement structures that contained large wooden shelves for bunks. In Auschwitz II-Birkenau, for example, there were 36 wooden bunks per barrack with five to six prisoners on a shelf. This enabled them to pack hundreds of prisoners in a barrack. There were blankets provided, but there was no insulation and the wooden roofs often leaked. A single bucket was provided as a toilet for the entire barrack. The prisoners slept in their clothes or on their clothes and shoes so they wouldn't be stolen. They were unable to stretch out and usually slept with arms and legs on another prisoner's body. There often was a stench due to horribly unsanitary conditions, and many prisoners became sick with dysentery and other illnesses. Sunday was not a workday, but the prisoners had to clean their barracks and take their weekly shower. Many, including my father and Moishe, eventually lost their teeth from decay due to the lack of dental hygiene or care while they were in the concentration camps and therefore required false teeth soon after the war. And my father and Uncle Moishe talked about how cold they often were in the camps.

At one point, my father and Uncle Moishe were sent to the Mauthausen-Gusen labor camp for a few days. They apparently went by cattle car because my Uncle Moishe told the story of how my father passed out in the car on the way to the Mauthausen camp, and a woman told Moishe to give my father urine as he needed to be hydrated and that was the only option available. So Moishe urinated in my father's mouth, and shortly afterwards, my father coughed and spit it out but he was revived.

Mauthausen is located 12 miles east of Linz in Upper Austria. It was one of the largest labor camps in the German-controlled part of Europe. Moishe's registration number in Mauthausen was *122690* and my father's number was *122691* (see picture from *Mauthausen Nummernbuch*).

On February 3, 1945, my father and Uncle Moishe were transferred to Neuengamme, a network of concentration camps in Northern Germany. The Neuengamme concentration camp had originally been established by the SS in Hamburg, Germany. It became a network of over 85 satellite camps. Over 100,000 prisoners came through the Neuengamme camp system, and the verified death toll there was 42,900. The Neuengamme labor camps were run according to the SS concept of *"vernichtung durch Arbeit"*, which translates to "extermination through labor." The prisoners died from difficult slave labor combined with the guards brutally beating inmates arbitrarily. In addition, the extremely unsanitary, inhumane and unhygienic conditions led to widespread disease. The food provided was often inedible, and hunger, along with dysentery, was prevalent. Although there were infirmaries in the main camp, admission to the hospital was almost always a death sentence.

My grandfather told me the story about how he became very

sick and underweight because he hadn't eaten in a while. He was taken to the infirmary, and he did not want to go because he rarely saw fellow prisoners return from there. But when he got there, he was examined by a doctor who recognized him from the town where they had both lived, and the doctor reassured him that he would keep him there a few days and that he would be deemed able to work. The doctor then broke my grandfather's fingernail so he could stay longer in the hospital in order to regain his strength and be deemed fit to work again.

There were five working labor camps in the area at that time. I do not know which of these camps they were in. The number of prisoners in the Neuengamme satellite camps varied. It could be anywhere from a dozen to several hundred prisoners, depending upon the jobs that were necessary. Prisoners continued to try to work outside the camps in order to possibly have an opportunity to find food or cigarettes or anything that could later be bartered in the labor camp. My father told us about one instance in which an officer asked who knew about working with electricity, and that they needed several workers for this job. My father raised his hand even though he had no idea how to fix anything electric. He also knew there were probably other volunteers who had no clue, either. He hoped that at least a few of the volunteers actually knew how to work with electricity so they could show the rest what to do. If you were lucky, there were more than a few who knew what to do.

Death March

As the Russians were moving closer towards Auschwitz, Heinrich Himmler, a *Reichsfuhrer* and one of the most powerful of Hitler's deputies, began ordering the evacuation of the concentration camps. He told the camp commanders that the Führer (Adolf Hitler) would hold each one of them personally responsible if any of the prisoners were discovered by the enemy. This was the beginning of the movement of prisoners west to concentration camps in Germany, such as Bergen-Belsen, Dachau, Buchenwald, Mauthausen and several others. The goal was to get rid of all evidence of the monstrous treatment of prisoners, most of them Jews. It meant murdering as many Jews as possible so there would be no eyewitnesses. In addition, the Nazis tried to destroy documentary evidence, as well as explicit evidence such as the camps themselves, especially the crematoria, gas showers and so on.

In March 1945, the prisoners from the Neuengamme satellite camps began to be moved to Bergen-Belsen. My father said he was in Neuengamme about six to eight weeks and in Bergen-Belsen for two. Thus, I believe he and Moishe along with hundreds of others were ordered to march to Bergen-Belsen sometime towards the end of March. They marched by foot for 50 kilometers (31 miles) from Hanover to Bergen-Belsen in the Lower Saxony region of Northern Germany. During the marches, there were SS units on execution detail who followed behind the marching prisoners to shoot and kill anyone who was lagging or unable to continue.

One of the most amazing stories my father recalled was when they were marching in the freezing temperatures after a brutal day of hard labor. Somebody had stolen his boots and left him with wooden clogs. He had managed to find a part of a thick paper bag and wrapped it around one of his feet, hoping for warmth. But as he was walking, the foot wrapped in the bag started hurting him to the point where he couldn't walk without excruciating pain. When he unwrapped the bag, his foot was full of blisters. It turned out he had found a bag of cement mix. Between the cold and sweat from his foot mixing with the remaining contents in the bag, the bag had hardened into small pieces of cement. He continued walking for a bit until he couldn't stand it any longer. He already had a huge boil on his neck, which was incredibly painful. Now his foot was killing him; he decided to run up to the wagon that contained some food and steal a piece of bread, so the officer would shoot him and the pain would be over. When the officer, a Ukrainian commander, shouted at him, my father said, "Kill me now!"

The officer told him, "You don't decide when you will die. I will be the one to decide when you die." He then put my father on the wagon.

Bergen-Belsen and the Liberation

My father and Moishe must have arrived in Bergen-Belsen at the very beginning of May 1945. The camp was extremely overcrowded due to the number of prisoners who had marched there or been brought in from other camps. It was built for 10,000 prisoners, and by April 1945 there were 60,000. Hunger and extremely unsanitary conditions led to massive outbreaks of typhus, dysentery and tuberculosis. This resulted in thousands of deaths just before the liberation of the camps by the Allies. My father was assigned to drag bodies to a giant hole to be buried, so the Allies would not find evidence of the cruelty in the camp.

Uncle Moishe later talked about how he and my father were both sick when they got to Bergen-Belsen but did not dare tell anyone. The Nazis killed prisoners who were sick and no longer useful.

When the liberation finally came, the prisoners were given food like bread and margarine. However, because my father and Moishe were sick, they couldn't initially eat anything. Uncle Moishe swears they were lucky because many of the prisoners who did eat got extremely sick, and some ended up dying.

On April 11, 1945, Himmler agreed to cede the camp without a fight. The following day an agreement was signed designating the area around the camp as a neutral zone. This gave the Germans time to burn records and kill more prisoners in an attempt to eradicate evidence. Four days later, on April 15, the British 11th Armored Division liberated Bergen-Belsen. They were horrified by what they found. The soldiers discovered close to 60,000 prisoners inside the camp, most of them half-starved and seriously ill. They also discovered 13,000 corpses.

My father could have easily been one of those 13,000 dead bodies. The day of or the day before the liberation, the huge boil on his neck was constantly throbbing and he had to turn his whole body if he needed to look to either side. When a Nazi soldier hit him with a rubber stick on the neck in an apparent effort to kill him, he remembers feeling sudden relief from the pain of the boil and he immediately passed out. It turned out that the boil may have saved his life because he woke up in a hospital a few days later. He weighed 48 kilos, about 105 pounds. He was in the hospital for several months while he was treated for malnourishment, typhus and other serious ailments. Uncle Moishe was also in the hospital—to be disinfected and treated for malnourishment. Afterwards, Moishe went to see my father in the hospital, and when he did, he could see how sick my father was, and he said, "It was the first time I cried." They had helped each other throughout their long ordeal, and seeing my father so sick was too much for Moishe. Years later, when my father died in 2017, Uncle Moishe said he didn't "only lose a brother, he was like my father and mother as well."

5

AFTER THE WAR

AFTER THE WAR, THE AREA NEAR Bergen-Belsen became a displaced person (DP) camp for thousands of Jews. They could not return to their former homes or simply refused to, and emigration to other countries was limited. In effect, they were persons without a country.

The survivors of the Bergen-Belsen concentration camp became the first residents of the DP camp that was located nearby. The British later burned down the prisoner barracks at Bergen-Belsen due to the rampant diseases spawned by the horribly unhygienic conditions. Emergency hospitals were set up by the British Army, British Red Cross and other entities. Within the first month, 29,000 survivors from Bergen-Belsen were moved to the emergency hospital, but despite the joint efforts to help them, almost half of them died. Indeed, two months after being rescued, 11,000 survivors of the concentration camp still needed emergency treatment. Making everything more challenging was the fact that supplies, including clothes and food, were still scarce in the immediate aftermath of the war due to the poor state of the British economy. Still, healthy survivors began to be voluntarily repatriated by the Allies—with the notable exception of Soviet citizens. The Soviet Union obtained consent from the Allies that their citizens would be sent back to the Soviet Union even against their will. As it turned out, Velky Berezny and the Transcarpathian areas had become part of the Soviet Union. Thus, my father and my uncle Moishe were in jeopardy of being repatriated to what was now Soviet territory. However, they discovered they would be able to emigrate to Sweden. On June 26, 1945, my father began his journey there and my uncle Moishe followed a few weeks later.

Sweden, 1945–1947

My father arrived in Gothenburg, the second largest city in Sweden, on July 24, 1945. I'm not sure how or when he first arrived in Sweden, only that he made it. Initially, he required hospitalization in Almhult (in northern Sweden) for several weeks due to typhus and water on the lungs. Unlike many other places, Sweden was allowing thousands of Jews to emigrate there, which explains how my father and Uncle Moishe were able to enter the country. Sweden had remained neutral during the war. But now, in the aftermath, it was showing sympathy for Holocaust survivors, giving them a place to restore their physical and mental health and to regain some measure of confidence in the human race.

At this point, my father was 18 and Moishe was 15. As far as I know, they lived and worked in Gothenburg, which is on the west coast of southwestern Sweden. The climate is mild throughout the year due to the influence of the Gulf Stream. My father worked in the Grand Hotel Palace, cleaning silverware and doing other odd jobs as well. One benefit of his working in the hotel was being able to eat for free in the hotel kitchen, which helped him save the money he was earning. My uncle Moishe, meanwhile, went to a vocational school and learned how to solder and weld. When Uncle Moishe first arrived in Sweden, he was looking for my father and asked around if anyone knew Wolf Farkas, which was my father's Yiddish name. One day he asked someone named Eisenfish if he knew his brother, Wolf. Eisenfish said he knew a Wolf, an unusual guy who traded chocolate for herring. Uncle Moishe exclaimed, "That's him!"

More important, in Sweden, my father and Moishe met other Holocaust survivors and began, in effect, to live again. They ate much better, were paid for their work and were able to send and receive letters. They established friendships that lasted the rest of their lives. My father met the person who would become his best friend, a fellow survivor named Joe Spiegel. Joe met his wife, Gilda, there. Our families eventually lived around the corner from each other in Kew Garden Hills, Queens, in New York. As for Moishe, he, too, met his best friend, a survivor named Alex. He and Moishe loved sports and became avid skiers, bowlers and moviegoers. So many lifelong friendships were formed in Sweden during this period, and as the years went by and everyone's lives took different paths, they would visit and stay with one another in the various places they eventually moved to. There are pictures of my father and Moishe in Sweden with their new friends, and it is striking how they were able to engage in the simple joy of being alive. It was incredibly important for all of them—each one a survivor—to have each other close by. Having others who had gone through and understood the trauma and losses suffered was incredibly important in helping each other to live again. That was very clear.

My father, like most survivors, was trying to determine if any of his other relatives had survived the Holocaust. Though he knew his mother and his three youngest siblings had been murdered in Auschwitz, he was searching for his father, two older sisters and other relatives who might have survived. There were newspapers with hundreds of ads placed by survivors looking for family members and friends. My father and Uncle Moishe would pore over these ads, hoping to see a familiar name. One day, Uncle Moishe was in the bathroom in the hotel where my father was working, and while in there, he spotted a newspaper on the floor. In it, he saw an ad placed by their father, Samuel Farkas, looking for any family members. My father immediately sent a letter to his father, who had gone back to Vilyatana and Velky Berezny to see if there were any family members who had survived. In the letter, my father told him that he and Moishe were in Sweden.

My father and Moishe were overjoyed to find out their father was alive. Unfortunately, my father also learned from my grandfather that his two older sisters had not survived. His oldest sister, Rivka, had married Bela Deutsch on March 26, 1940. He was 29 and described as a "Talmud student," and she was 19. She was pregnant when they were deported to the labor camps. The story I was always told is that she died in childbirth—which really may have meant she lost the baby and her own life due to the horrific conditions in the camps. Her sister Sarah then died of a "broken heart," which probably meant losing the will to live. Dr. Victor Frankl, who was a Holocaust survivor and renowned psychologist, said the quest to find meaning in one's life was a central tenet of existence. For some Holocaust survivors, finding meaning meant locating other family members who also survived. For other survivors, it was to bear witness to what had occurred. I believe for my father and uncle, as well as for Rivka and Sarah, it was to help each other. When Rivka died in childbirth, Sarah lost, not just her sister, but also her purpose. In general, research indicates those who worked together and helped each other during the Holocaust fared better than those who looked out only for themselves.

In the end, out of a family of nine with seven children, my father, Moishe and my grandfather were the only survivors. Back home, where my grandfather had gone to see if anyone had returned, he found his house occupied by strangers, as were most houses owned by Jewish families prior to the deportations. He knew there was nothing he could do about it. My father also learned from my grandfather that the only person who seemingly survived from the families of my grandfather's eight siblings was a cousin, Bruchela, who was the daughter of my grandfather's second oldest sibling, Bayla. She went on to settle in Marseilles, France. He also learned my mother's family was in Belgium. Later on, he and Moishe and my grandfather discovered two other cousins who had survived the concentration camps, Avrum and Tzaler Farkas, sons of my grandfather's oldest sister, Sarah, who settled in Brooklyn. Many years later, my father learned of two other cousins, Wolf Farkas, his Uncle Shlomo's son, and Hencha, his Aunt Yita's daughter, who had also survived. Thus, from a family of well over 60 members, only 12 survived the war.

Actually, it was only in 1979 that we learned that Wolf Farkas, who was named after the same grandfather as my father, had been allowed to emigrate to Israel by the Soviet Union. It was only then that our families learned of each other's survival. Wolf had married and had two sons, Shlomo and Avrom Meir, who had served in the

Soviet army. In Israel, the family settled in Migdal Emek. Both sons married and had children there. Our two families saw each other for the first time in the summer of 1979, when my parents, paternal grandfather and maternal grandmother; my sister, Brenda; my wife, Sue; and I all went to Israel.

Here were Holocaust survivors who had been able to build new lives and families thousands of miles apart and were now finally coming together. What they had in common despite leading such different lives since the war was that they had been able to suppress the trauma they had undergone in order to embrace the future. Many could not do this, but luckily my parents were among those resilient enough to be able to build a new family and home together. In fact, in Dr. William Helmreich's study of Holocaust survivors in the United States, he found that four out of five who made it through the Holocaust married other survivors. Marrying another survivor was often important as it enabled both persons to talk about what happened to them with somebody who would understand. Furthermore, these marriages turned out to be very stable. When Dr. Helmreich's study was done in 1989, 83 percent of the survivors he talked with were still married, compared to 62 percent of other American Jews of the same age.

While the survivors wanted to move on and live their lives, it wasn't that simple. There were experiences they had gone through and been witness to which could not be easily erased and forgotten. Ten years after the war, when my uncle Moishe lived with us in Brooklyn, I can recall him having nightmares. They were often about a particular time when he was hiding from the Nazi soldiers and rats were all around him. In the immediate aftermath of the war, the Red Cross and other agencies were helping the survivors regain their physical health, but nobody was really thinking about their mental and emotional well-being. For sure, my father and Uncle Moishe's inability to properly mourn the loss of their mother and five siblings, and then the need to push past the sustained trauma of what they had endured, could only be dealt with among their friends who had shared the same horrors. The psychiatric community was not reaching out to them in those years. Thus, the survivors only had one another. As I noted earlier, when I was growing up, I did eavesdrop on my parents' conversations when their friends, all of whom were survivors, would get together. They were the only ones who could really understand what they had gone through.

To illustrate how much my parents had to hold in just to be able to live productive lives, years later, around 1993, we went as a multigenerational family to visit the Holocaust Museum in Washington, D.C. Our group consisted of my parents, Sue and I, our children Elissa and Eric, and my cousin Carole from France, who was related through the Sobel family on my father's maternal side. During the several hours we were there, we moved through the exhibits quietly, and there was little talking among us. This was true for all the visitors there, as it is a very solemn and somber experience. Afterwards, my father stated how being in the museum was a very intense experience for him, especially encountering the cattle car that was part of the overall exhibit. He said the car smelled the same as it had over 50 years before, and he got choked up as he was describing it.

A few minutes later, as we were leaving, we noticed an exhibit created for children called *Daniel's Story*. It was about a young Jewish boy in Germany and how his life had changed under Nazi rule. It was designed so that we would walk from one room to another in a circular manner as we followed Daniel's story. Eric had learned to read by this time, and he read the short synopsis on each wall. It starts with Daniel being the younger brother who is learning to play piano in his house. Afterwards, he cannot go to school with his friends. Next, he is huddled with his family in a small room in the ghetto with barely anything to sustain them. Finally, he is sent to a concentration camp, where he doesn't make it out alive.

At that point, we were back in the hallway of the museum. All of a sudden Eric and Elissa started to cry, and within seconds we were all crying, huddled together, hugging as we were sobbing, especially my mom and my dad, who hardly ever cried. It was an incredible moment when the experience of the Holocaust was suddenly being shared by three generations and my parents were able to give release to emotions that had mostly gone unexpressed for so long.

The Nazis had aimed to eradicate the Jewish race—and beyond that, to eliminate all traces of Jewish culture, or what they termed the "*Judischer Geist*" (Jewish spirit/mind). In this, they almost succeeded, at least when it came to the Jewish population in Europe. Prior to World War II, an estimated 11 million Jews were living in thousands of communities, large and small, throughout Europe. More than half of that population died in the Holocaust. The Yiddish-based Ashkenazi communities of rural cities like Velky Berezny, and the smaller towns and shtetls like Vilyatana in Transcarpathia, where Jews had lived for generations, all but disappeared. Of further note, consider that my father was 17 and my uncle Moishe 14 when they entered the ghetto and the concentration camps, while my mother was 13, my aunt Regina 9, and my uncle Victor only 8 months old when they left their parents to be hidden in the convent/orphanage. As I noted earlier, in Nazi-occupied Europe, 1.5 million Jewish children were exterminated (including my father's three youngest siblings); barely 100,000 survived. It's nothing short of a miracle that my mother and her siblings, as well as my father and Uncle Moishe, did.

Belgium (1947–1952)

In the summer of 1947, my father decided to go to Liege, Belgium, to visit his relatives there. He was very young when his family left Vilyatana, and he really did not remember his aunt and uncle (my maternal grandparents) nor had he ever met his cousins. Esther was almost 18, Regine was 14 and Victor was 6 years old. They welcomed him, and he stayed with them. My father was introduced to various tailors who took him under their wings and taught him a great deal. He learned quickly and became quite proficient. He told me he was making robes for priests in one of the tailor's shops. That experience later enabled him to make the long black silk coats (*bekitches*) for the Hasidim who lived in the area. Meanwhile, there was an immediate attraction between my parents. My father said that he fell in love with my mother as soon as he saw her. She must have felt the same because after a while, her father told both of them it looked like they were "acting like lovebirds and if they were serious, get married and get a job." They *were* serious, and they were married at City Hall on November 4, 1948; the religious ceremony took place in my grandparents' apartment on January 6, 1949, the date they used to celebrate their wedding anniversary during every year of their marriage. Jewish law permits marriages between cousins, and this was especially true after the Holocaust, as the rabbis wanted to rebuild the Jewish community after so many had died.

My parents' life in Liege was simple, and they were surrounded by family, as well as friends. These friends had an unbreakable bond with my parents—they were all survivors—and they remained lifelong friends. Meanwhile, my parents rented a lovely apartment a few blocks from my grandparents on rue Hennet, one room of which was dedicated to my father's business. He always had at least one or two people working with him. The room had a sewing machine and a large table so he could cut the material from the patterns he made. My mother helped out, as she was a seamstress.

They later moved to an apartment closer to my grandparents with a view of the river—*la Meuse*. Finally, because that apartment was expensive, they moved again, this time across the street from my grandparents. One room in the apartment remained my father's tailoring room. At that point, my aunt Regine was still living with my grandparents, as was Victor.

On March 24, 1950, I was born. I was the first grandchild in the family, and everyone was excited as the rebuilding of what had been lost was very important. My parents were in touch with my grandfather, who was still in Transcarpathia, trying to restart his life. He had begun working in the Carpathian Mountains for the Hungarian government. He was in constant touch with his sister in Belgium and appeared to be doing well financially, as he often sent them packages. He had also remarried. However, his second wife, whose name was Elsa, was ill, and he requested medicines from my grandparents in Belgium that he could not obtain in Czechoslovakia. Unfortunately, Elsa died not too long after their marriage, and my grandfather became a widower for the second time.

He was sent word of my birth and immediately decided he would leave Czechoslovakia and travel to Liege to see his new grandson. Due to the fact that I was underweight, it was decided that my *bris* would not be on the eighth day after my birth. It was agreed instead that it would be the same day as my *pidyon haben* (redemption of the first-born mitzvah), a month after my birth. As a result, my grandfather was able to attend the bris and was given the honor of being my *kvater* (godfather), or the one who carries the child from the mother to the father, who then carries him to the *mohel*. Having children is the biggest mitzvah in Judaism. This was especially so after the Holocaust and the murder of six million Jews, which destroyed so many families. The rebuilding of *"Klal Yisrael"* (the Jewish People) was and still is a huge mitzvah among Orthodox Jews.

My father continued to work from the apartment. He had a good number of customers, and he would travel to their homes and take their measurements. They would pick out the material from the swatches he had, and he would then make them the suits, jackets, pants, or coats they had ordered. He made a good living, and the fact that my mother and father were living across the street from my maternal grandparents and aunt and uncle made it feel somewhat like the pre-war days in Czechoslovakia, when family was always nearby. Nevertheless, my father realized neither he nor my mother would ever be citizens of Belgium since they hadn't been born there. He also had to engage in his business somewhat secretly, as non-citizens could not own shops or stores. As a result, he wanted to move to the United States, so he could eventually become a citizen there and have more opportunities.

My mother, on the other hand, did not want to leave her family in Liege. She had been separated from them under harrowing circumstances during the war, and while she understood my father's concerns and desires, she was not ready to move. When he kept asking, she told him to apply for a visa, just so he would stop asking. She knew it would take quite a while, as there were quotas and many Holocaust survivors were filling out applications to emigrate to the United States, including some of their friends.

Still, however long it was going to take, my father needed a sense of belonging and the knowledge that he could have his own business. In addition, after what he and my mother had gone through during the Holocaust, he found it hard to believe that living in Europe would ever really be safe for Jews.

Meanwhile, when my paternal grandfather came to Belgium for my *bris*, he was introduced through a friend of my maternal grandparents, a woman named Madame Pik, to her cousin, a widow named Fella Pik *née* Felicie Zammel. She lived in Metz, France. Within a year, my grandfather and Fella Pik were married. She was seven years older than my grandfather and had a wholesale clothing store, which had fallen into decline after her husband passed away. But my grandfather quickly learned the business, figuring out which clothing would sell and which wouldn't and, as a result, the store flourished and they were able to live comfortably. Shortly thereafter, around 1952, my grandfather sent money so that my uncle Moishe, who was still in Sweden, could come to Metz. He was now reunited with his father and stayed with him and his wife.

Several weeks later, Moishe came to visit our family in Liege, where he was reunited with my father, who he hadn't seen for almost five years. He stayed with my parents for several weeks and told them he was not really happy living in Metz. My father spoke to him about emigrating to the United States and Moishe said he, too, would apply for a visa. He returned to Metz and was in touch with his friends in Sweden and they were also keen on the idea of starting a new life in the United States.

My mother would always describe these years in Liege as fulfilling. She was married and had a baby. Her husband was doing well and loving what he was doing. She was able to help him since my grandparents and Aunt Regine were across the street and were able to take care of me. After all they had been through, my parents now had family nearby, jobs they enjoyed and friends with whom to share their good fortune. More than anything, they had each other, and since I was the only child and grandchild, I was doted on. I often joke that I was so different than my brother, Eddie, and my sister, Brenda, because my grandparents showered me with so much affection during those early years in Belgium. Or perhaps I was adopted. Actually, I am certain it is the former.

During this period, life continued to go well for my parents and grandparents. Aunt Regine was often meeting arranged suitors seeking her hand in marriage. She agreed to marry Benny Neuman, who was almost 10 years older than her. She was 18 at the time. He and his family had lived in Ganitsh (Yiddish pronunciation—it is Hanyci in Ukrainian), which is in southern Transcarpathia, 24 miles east of Khust. Benny had survived the death and labor camps in Dachau and Buchenwald. His father died before World War II, and his mother, Etya, sold dry goods from town to town. As a result, Benny and his siblings lived with an uncle who had 10 children of his own. Uncle Benny and his siblings were deported to the death and labor camps in 1944. Benny managed to stay alive, as did his brother, Yosi, who emigrated to Jerusalem, and his sister, Eida, who emigrated to London. As for Benny, after the war, he was sponsored by a family in Antwerp, Belgium, and emigrated there. It was through them that a meeting with Aunt Regine was arranged. He had also applied for a visa to the United States from the Polish Consulate well prior to their wedding. On his visa application he declared himself a displaced person, and his visa came through shortly after the wedding. It was agreed he would emigrate, and that once he was able to do so, he would send money for Aunt Regine to come. Benny had become a tailor and he had a friend in Dallas who was a tailor and was confident he could get him a job there. So, Benny left Belgium for Dallas and lived with his friend Fishel, his wife, Lola, and their children. Regine would follow soon after. Uncle Benny was adept at telling a story or a joke that would make people howl with laughter. Aunt Regine was sweet and loving and was a great audience for Uncle Benny. They made a great couple as he could run the show and she was always agreeable and supportive of his decisions.

6

THE MOVE TO AMERICA

Dallas (1952–1953)

TOWARD THE END OF 1952, MY FATHER FOUND out his visa from the Czechoslovakian Embassy had come through. He had applied as a DP (displaced person) and thus been given given priority, like many other DPs. He told my mother, who was surprised but still not happy about leaving Belgium to go across the ocean to a country she didn't know anything about. But my father felt they would never be granted citizenship in Belgium and without that status he would never be able to own his own business, which he very much wanted to do. And as I previously noted, he was wary of remaining in Europe. In any case, after some discussion and several postponements, my parents had to make a decision—either to emigrate or be taken off the list. My mother agreed to go, which in turn created a lot of difficult moments for my grandparents, especially my grandmother, who often was in tears.

While my mother was reluctant to go, she was happy that her sister would be going as well. Benny was already there and could get my father a job in the place that he worked. My parents packed up and we left on the *SS United States* on November 7, 1952, setting sail from Le Havre, France, and arriving in New York City four and a half days later. The *SS United States* was the first, and largest, ocean liner built entirely in the United States. It was also the fastest transatlantic liner at that time, and its maiden voyage had occurred just several months before we boarded the ship. I was 2 years old at the time. We came to New York and met my father's cousins, Avrum and his wife, Olga; and Tzaler and his wife, Malchy (Malka). Tzaler and Malchy had two children, Moishe Shmiel and Suri. They were only a few years older than me.

After a short stay in New York, we went to Dallas, where a job was indeed waiting for my father. I often think about the tremendous uncertainty my parents must have felt during this period, arriving in a new country with a different language and a different culture. They only knew a few people in a tremendously large nation that was as big as all of Europe. But they had hope for a better future, and they had each other.

They had also arrived in New York with just $80.00 and had to travel to Dallas and still have enough money to pay $50.00 in rent for a place to live. They figured out a way to do it, though, and our apartment was near where Uncle Benny lived, along with Benny's friend Fishel and his family.

Although we had our own apartment, the kitchen and bathroom were shared with the other tenants in the complex. Once in

Dallas, my father started working the next day at Model Tailors. He commuted by bus, and one story I remember my father telling me was about getting on the bus and going to sit in the back, only to find other passengers staring at him. He felt uncomfortable and couldn't understand why everyone was staring. He wondered if they knew he was Jewish and were prejudiced against him. When he got home and told Fishel what had happened, his friend explained that only black people were supposed to sit in the back of the bus. My father asked why that was the case and was told that white people did not want to sit with black people. He was taken aback to learn that. He had gone through so much because the Nazis had decided Jews were less than human beings and could be murdered or used as slave labor just because they were Jewish. Now he was discovering that there was racial bigotry in the United States. It was his first lesson about prejudice in this country, and it made him sad.

In general, it was hard for my parents to learn a new language and new culture. Thankfully, they had Uncle Benny and Fishel and Lola and their children, who became my playmates. We all lived on the same block, with the grown-ups speaking Yiddish with one another, and Aunt Regine arriving in Dallas just a few months after us.

There was a Jewish community in Dallas, so my father had a synagogue to attend and meet other people as well. My mother had a more difficult time because she was missing her parents. She described this initial time period in the United States as "feeling lost." She swore she would save up money and go back to Belgium to visit her parents and family as soon as she and my father became American citizens, which would take five years from their arrival in the United States.

Brooklyn-Williamsburg (1953–1958)

We stayed in Dallas for six months and then moved to Williamsburg in Brooklyn to settle near family who were already living there. My parents also had other friends from the "old country" who had settled in Brooklyn. The synagogues there were like the ones in Vilyatana and Velky Berezny, and my parents began to feel more comfortable. They said it was more *"heimish,"* or homey, in Brooklyn than in Dallas, and Benny and Regine would soon follow as well. Fetter Avrum and Uncle Tzaler found an apartment for my parents that was very close to them. Our apartment was at 538 Willoughby Avenue, on the second floor of a three-story walk-up brownstone. The apartment was bigger than the one in Dallas, and we had our own kitchen and bathroom. The building was owned by the Musiker family, who lived on the first floor. The Teper family lived on the third floor. A black family lived on the ground floor, and they had a son named Junior. He and I played in the front of the house, as we were close in age. He was my first friend in Brooklyn.

Several months later, Uncle Benny and Aunt Regine came, and with everyone living in easy walking distance of one another, there were a lot of family get-togethers. Yiddish would be the primary language spoken although my mother and Aunt Regine spoke French to each other. As I noted earlier, I remember playing board games with Moishe Shmiel and Suri, and we collected stamps and had stamp albums. We also collected pennies and had the book in which you could put in pennies from each year. I really enjoyed visiting with them; we always had fun together.

There was and still is a vibrant Orthodox Jewish community in Williamsburg. My father and I went to the local Orthodox synagogue, and Fetter Avrum, Uncle Tzaler and Moishe Shmiel went to the Hasidic Satmar *shul*, which was even more Orthodox.

When we first arrived in Brooklyn, my father had been told about a possible job in the garment district in Manhattan. He learned how to take the subway from Brooklyn to Manhattan, got on the train and got the job. And that evening he passed a local tailor shop near our apartment owned by a man named Mr. Edelman. My father went into the shop and proceeded to get a part-time job working at night and on Sunday. So, on his first day, with very limited knowledge of English, he had gotten two jobs as a tailor, which was pretty amazing.

The first job was at Goodstein Bros., where he made suits from patterns he would cut. The Garment Center was thriving at that time, and there were hundreds of small companies employing many immigrants who were tailors. Thus, the workplace often had many languages being spoken in the course of a day. My father had the ability to learn languages quickly, so he got along well with everyone. He spoke some Czech, German, Hungarian, Russian, French and of course Yiddish, and meanwhile he was learning English. People, especially Jews, referred to working in the garment center as working in the *"schmatta"* business. *Schmatta*, in Yiddish, means "rag."

In Mr. Edelman's store, my father altered men's and women's clothing and cut patterns for suits. Sometimes, I would go to work with him on Sunday, and sometimes my mother and I would both visit him there.

Mr. Edelman also spoke Yiddish and would ask me questions and always give me a dime or a quarter when I left the store. I liked him and always asked my mother to go visit *"tatti"* (which is Yiddish for "daddy" and was what I called my father).

My father was working very hard so he could pay the bills and save money to eventually go into business for himself. He would come home, eat dinner, and then go to Mr. Edelman's store a few blocks away. After Mr. Edelman left the shop, my father would close up when he was done.

Writing about Mr. Edelman reminded me of Mrs. Brenda, a plump, elderly neighbor who had braided white hair and a nice smile. My parents stopped to talk to her when she was outside the building. When we moved a few years later, I remember visiting her in a nursing home and also visiting Mr. Edelman when his wife died. My parents were respectful of the elderly, maybe because they wanted surrogate parents in a new country or because they left their own parents at such a young age. However, I saw them be like that throughout their lives, especially when my father had his own store and when my mother worked in the nursing home. They always showed respect for those who were older although it was never spoken about.

My mother liked Brooklyn and being close to family, but over all, it was still hard for her. She was alone with a child, and a new language and culture. She went to school to learn English while I went to the nursery downstairs.

I was still very young but I do not remember feeling uneasy about anything during those years. My dad was working two jobs and we always had what we wanted and were surrounded by family. I recall going to stores with my mother to shop and taking walks to our relatives. She seemed invariably to be in a positive mood. She told me years later that she didn't want us to have the fears she'd had growing up, so she put up a good front.

Another example of this occurred when we went to the bungalow colonies in the Catskill Mountains. She would insist I learn to swim in the lake and later told me she was had always been afraid of drowning and didn't want her children to be afraid. While she'd had to learn the subway and bus systems without having mastered English, she did not want me to have that problem. She wanted me to speak English. I remember often translating words from English into Yiddish or even French. Eventually, I was fluent in English and Yiddish, but my French faded as I wasn't using it much anymore.

During these years in Williamsburg, our family grew. My brother, Eddie, was born on January 17, 1954. We shared a room, and I remember him being small and skinny. In addition, he had various physical and health issues. He was pigeon-toed and required inserts in his special shoes. He also had weak knees and, as a result, was not very athletic. He also had terrible nosebleeds, which frequently required doctor visits and, once, an emergency room visit. The nosebleeds eventually disappeared, but his pigeon-toed feet and weak knees remained throughout his life. In addition, he had crippling headaches as an adult and was hospitalized several times due to their severity, with no relief provided from a variety of medications. All of this gave him a physical fragility, but he was incredibly stoic and rarely complained.

The same year that Eddie was born, Uncle Moishe emigrated to the United States via his Displaced Person status. He proudly noted that he had arrived on a Monday and started a job on Tuesday. He worked in the tool-and-die trade and lived with us for several months until he was able to get his own apartment with his best friend, Alex.

Aunt Regine and Uncle Benny were starting a family as well. Ethel was born a year after Eddie and Moishe (Morris) a few years later, in 1958. Since we all lived near one another, it was easy for the two families to get together, first in Williamsburg and then when we moved to Bensonhurst. Our apartment was the place where we celebrated the holidays with our families and friends. My mother did all the cooking and assumed the role of matriarch of the family. This went on even after my parents were in their 70s, at which point their grandchildren were present.

During these early family years, we started going to a bungalow colony called Siegelman's in the Catskill Mountains. A bungalow colony was a place where many families rented either a room or a bungalow (a cottage) for the summer. Siegelman's was located in Cuddebackville, near Port Jervis. Going on vacation was an American concept because vacations did not exist for Jews in the *shtetls* of Eastern Europe. When we were headed to Siegelman's, we used to say we were "going to the country," because the area was green, mountainous and lush. In general, there were a lot of Jews who vacationed in this area because they weren't all that welcomed in many other places.

In fact, I later learned the mountains the Jews vacationed in were not actually in the Catskills but in the Shawangunk Mountains because the actual Catskills communities were not that happy with Jews spending time there, whether it was vacationing or eating in local restaurants or just buying gas.

Thus, the Shawangunk Mountains became known as the Jewish Catskills. The first few years we went there in the summer, we stayed in what was called the Main House, which had two or three floors with separate two-room apartments per floor. Eventually, we rented our own two-room bungalow. There were a lot of kids to play with and it was nothing like Brooklyn, as there was a huge, all-grass baseball field, rows of corn growing behind the field—from which we picked ears of corn to have for dinner—and a waterfall within hiking distance. We had a lot of fun and while the grounds were vast, you could always see if there were any kids out playing. There was a telephone in the casino—a community room of sorts—from which you could make or receive calls. We would watch television in the casino and, on Saturday night, televised wrestling with many of the fathers. I can still remember the names of some of the wrestlers—Bruno Sammartino, Bobo Brazil and Haystacks Calhoun. There were also dances in the casino for the adults later at night.

My parents, Eddie and I initially traveled to Siegelman's with a hired driver since neither of my parents knew how to drive. Late Sunday night, my father returned to Brooklyn on the train, or with another father by car, and then come back to Siegelman's the following Friday afternoon.

I remember waiting, along with all the other kids, for our dads to arrive. They usually brought us something when they came, nothing big but something. I can recall getting thin airplane gliders made out of balsa wood that I would put together and that only lasted a day or two, a water pistol that we used all summer, a cheap bow-and-arrow set with rubber darts that could stick to a wall. I loved these small gifts and it seemed we all got something similar.

My father would also take two weeks of vacation and stay at Siegelman's the entire time. That was the best. All of the families in the bungalow colony lived either in Brooklyn or the Bronx, and all had at least one parent who was a Holocaust survivor. Most were married to other Holocaust survivors. Almost all the children went to yeshiva, like I did. Those days were probably the closest we came to what it must have been like living in Vilyatana, where you knew everybody and everyone spoke Yiddish and usually greeted you with a smile. On Saturdays in the summer, we all went to *shul* in the casino. For several years during that period, Aunt Regine and

Uncle Benny came to Siegelman's with Ethel and Morris. The same families came every year, and our families remained friends even when we stopped going to Siegelman's in the summer. Several members of this group moved to Israel or Florida in their later years, but everyone remained in touch.

I used to tell my children that my dad never threw a ball or played any kind of sports with me or my brother, but neither did anybody else's parents at the bungalow colony or in Brooklyn. In fact, none of the parents ever really learned the rules or understood the game of baseball or football. My mother and the other mothers would watch us when we played a baseball team from another bungalow colony. I don't think they ever really knew what was going on, since they only talked to one another and often asked afterward if we'd won the game. In any case, playing ball all the time in the bungalow colony was different than in the city because we had enough kids to have a full team, which we never did in Brooklyn. Even more amazing was playing on grass as opposed to the concrete baseball fields in the local parks back home.

Citizenship and Visit to Belgium and France (1958)

Almost five years to the day after we arrived in the United States, my mother passed the test and received her citizenship papers on January 28, 1958. My dad and I received our citizenship papers several months later. We were now naturalized citizens of the United States. A month later, on February 28, my mother applied for passports so we could visit her parents and her brother, Victor, in Belgium, as well as my paternal grandfather in France. We were scheduled to leave right after school was over.

I attended kindergarten in Brooklyn Yeshiva, which was in our neighborhood in Williamsburg. I then moved on to Yeshiva Chasam Sofer on the Lower East Side in Manhattan. I would take a school bus across the Williamsburg Bridge to get to the yeshiva and went to school until 5:00 p.m. every day, with Hebrew studies in the morning and English studies after lunch.

Meanwhile, four days before we were to depart for Belgium on Sabena Airlines, I was running a fever and was diagnosed with German measles, with a rash all over my body. We were all worried whether my fever would break and I would be able to fly. Luckily, my fever broke the day before we were scheduled to depart and everyone was relieved. My father stayed home because he had to work. My mother, my brother and I flew to Brussels and then took a train to Liege. We were met by my grandfather, whom I recognized from pictures but really did not remember. I was 8 years old and Eddie was 4. My grandfather was so happy to see us and couldn't stop smiling even though my mother was crying from the sheer emotion of the reunion.

After a short trip, we arrived at my grandparents' apartment on rue Matthieu Polan. It was the same apartment that they had been living in when we left Belgium, and several neighbors came to greet us. They remembered my mother and noted how much I had grown since we left. My grandmother had food ready, and we ate and talked. There were questions about the flight, about school, about the United States and about my dad. Victor was not there because he had enlisted in the army to learn to become an engineer. My most vivid recollection of the apartment, which was very small, was a chandelier—really just three light bulbs with pretty red shades—that Victor had made. My grandfather proudly pointed it out.

My grandmother was not at all pleased with Victor's decision to go into the army. She hated the army uniform and anything to do with the army due to her horrible experiences during the war. I would soon find out more about those experiences and eventually understand her difficulty with uniforms and Nazis.

I can recall trips during that visit that I took with my grandfather to the town citadel and to various parks where I played with the children who were there. He was always so proud to take my brother and me places where he could show us off to his friends, especially when we went to synagogue and he asked me to show everyone how I was able to *daven* ("pray" in Hebrew). I remember, too, that my mother took us to a Russian circus set up in the Place de Lise, which was a few blocks from the apartment. We also went to the World's Fair in Brussels.

At some point, we left to take the train to Metz, France, to visit my paternal grandfather. When we left, I saw my grandmother crying, and my mother reassured her we would be back in a week. When we got to Metz, my *zeide* (grandfather) met us at the train station and we walked to his apartment. We met his wife, whom my mother called *tante* (aunt). She had a nice smile, but I recall her being stern and making my brother and me sit quietly at the table when they served food. She wasn't as sweet and loving as my grandmother in Belgium, who was always asking us if we wanted more food or something to drink.

We had our own apartment in Metz, two floors above them in the same building. It was much larger and nicer than my grandparents' apartment in Liege, which I loved because it was so cozy. My grandfather showed me his library of "*sforim*" and his "*Shas*" (Hebrew books and a set of the Talmud). When we went to *shul*, I could tell he was greatly respected and looked up to. He *davened* for the congregation, making him the cantor, and I was proud to be his grandson. We had a good visit with my grandfather and I would see him many more times in the future, but this was the only time I ever saw my step-grandmother.

We took the train back to Liege, and when we got there my grandfather told us that my grandmother wasn't home. She was sick and had to go to the hospital. Nothing more about it was said except for my mother telling me I would go with her the next day to visit my "Babi," which is what I called my grandmother. "*Bubbe*" is Yiddish for "grandmother," but we pronounced it "Babi." My brother would stay home with my grandfather since he was too young to visit. The next day, as we left to walk to the bus stop, my mother told me that my grandmother might not look good due to her illness and I should not be upset if that were the case. I was also told repeatedly not to cry in front of her.

When we got off the bus and walked towards the entrance of the hospital, my mother again reminded me not to cry because it would upset my grandmother. As we walked in, I saw nurses in their white uniforms and nuns in their white habits. I can recall the smell of something like ether or some other medicinal odor. When I think of this story, I can still smell that hospital.

We were shown where my grandmother's bed was—the fourth bed against the wall once we turned the corridor from the entrance. As we got closer, my grandmother saw us and cried out to me, "*Hershela, ratta mich fin do*" ("Heshy, save me from here"), and I immediately started sobbing. So much for no crying. My grandmother wanted out, and even as a child that was clear to me, but I didn't understand what was wrong with her.

After we left, my mother explained that my grandmother was very sick because she missed us and was afraid that we would not return. I didn't quite understand that either, but years later realized that she had had a nervous breakdown and that it wasn't the first time, either. It turned out that she'd had several episodes that began when she was going through menopause, which was shortly after my family first left for the United States.

My grandfather and my uncle Victor had been dealing with this situation off and on, and I later learned my grandmother was suffering from psychotic depression and was getting shock treatments. I fully realized the severity of all this when she came to live with us after my grandfather died in 1970. My grandmother's depression was triggered any time that people she loved left her. It probably reminded her of the two times in her life when she had to send her three children to the convent/orphanage to save them from the Nazis. These horrific abandonment issues never left her and plagued her for much of the rest of her life.

I consider that trip to the hospital a seminal moment in my life in shaping who I am. It was a microcosm of my parents' inability to fully express the normal emotions of sadness, frustration and anger. At the hospital, the message had been very clear: "Don't cry." As I grew up, this message was much less overt, but it was still there. My mother had difficulty listening to us complain, and I didn't want to cause more aggravation for my father after everything he had gone through in the Holocaust. So I, as well as my brother and sister, learned to often cope silently and take care of things ourselves. As a result, as a parent, I was determined to allow my children to express any and all emotions. I can recall my wife, Sue, and I talking to my mother when she once told Elissa, "Don't be a baby," when she was still a toddler. We told my mother this was unacceptable.

My grandmother returned home a few days after our visit to

the hospital, and it took a while before she was her old self. Still, we continued to enjoy the rest of our time together. Victor would come and stay for a few days but then head back to his job with the army. He never wore his uniform when he was home. As the summer ended, we had to return to New York because school would start soon. When we landed in New York, my mother called my father at a phone booth. As it turned out, she needed to get our new address, since he had found a new place for us to live while we were in Belgium. Like many others that we knew, my parents had decided to move out of Williamsburg. Fetter Avrum and Mimi ("aunt" in Hungarian) Olga as well as Uncle Tzaler, Tante Malchy, Moishe Shmiel and Suri moved to Borough Park. Uncle Benny and Aunt Regine moved to a house in Canarsie. We moved to 6813 21st Avenue in Bensonhurst, into an apartment on the fourth floor of a walk-up building. It was bigger than our previous apartment because it had a much larger foyer, which my father would use as a place for a sewing machine. The living room was also bigger. My brother and I shared a room that was larger as well. This would not be the last time my parents wouldn't tell us before we moved. As a result, Sue and I always prepared our children for changes, and they participated. For example, our daughter, Elissa, helped paint the bookshelves when we moved from Manhattan to our house in Plainview, Long Island. Elissa and Eric would choose the toys they wanted when we went on vacations.

Bensonhurst (1958–1967)

I was then enrolled in Yeshiva Beer Shmuel in Borough Park, but I only went there for one year. The following one, Eddie started kindergarten and we went to Yeshiva Ohel Yacov. It was about seven blocks from our apartment, and my mother would walk us there, then visit with Phyllis Vegh, who lived with her parents about a block from the yeshiva. Phyllis was from England, as were her parents, so they sounded particularly smart when they spoke. As it was, I was used to hearing people from the old country speak English with an accent. Phyllis was married to Maurice Vegh, who was a Holocaust survivor and came from the same area in Transcarpathia as my parents. We also lived near Biji and Gabriel Kaczor, who owned a candy store down the block from us. They were also Holocaust survivors who came from my parents' town. They, along with Biji's sisters Goldie and Sidie and their husbands, became lifelong friends of my parents. And I was friends with their children, especially Harry and Benny Kaczor. My mother often said that because we had lost so much family, our friends became family. Their friends must have felt similarly since they, too, had lost so much family. It is also why friends mean so much to Sue and me. Our children grew up with our friends, both near and far, being a big part of their lives throughout their childhood.

My parents were not happy with the school Eddie and I were attending, so they registered us at Yeshiva Toras Emes. Eddie started first grade, and I was in fifth. It was my fifth school in six years. I spent the next three years in Toras Emes and made friends that would last through high school. I realized where we lived was pretty far from most things in my life. My school was in Borough Park, which meant I had to take two trains and two short walks in order to get there. This was 1960; I was only 10, and my brother was 6. We walked a few blocks from our house, crossed a major street, Bay Parkway, to get to the Sea Beach Line (now the N train), took it three stops to New Utrecht Avenue, and walked upstairs to the West End Line (now the QB train) for another three stops. We then had to walk to the school, which was on 43rd Street and 13th Avenue. It would now be unthinkable for children as young as we were to do all this without adults. But it was a different time, and I met other friends at the train station who were going to the yeshiva with us.

Many of my friends lived at least a mile from us, and on Shabbos, I always walked to their homes. Most of them lived between 81st Street and the Bay, which was over a mile from our apartment. The Bay was a body of water along the Belt Parkway off Bay Parkway. We would go to the park there and walk along the walkway by the water below the Verrazano Bridge, which was being built at the time. From our apartment window, you could actually see the bridge being constructed in the distance. The area along the Bay included several baseball fields as well as tennis courts. On sunny days, the water would glisten, and the green grass, along with the sandlot fields, made everything seem so alive and yet peaceful. Sometimes, I would walk to the homes of other friends who lived in Borough Park, but we mostly hung out by the Bay. I attended all-boys yeshivas, but several of my friends attended Yeshiva Ohel Moshe, which was a co-ed school. My first two girlfriends in high school were from this group. During my freshman year, I met Elke. Her brother went to school with me, and she was a year younger than us. We were together for about a year. Faygie was my second girlfriend; we were together about two years. It was all very innocent, holding hands and hugging, but it was real and very gratifying at the time.

An interesting story occurred during this period. I was always called Heshy by my family, but in high school, I was called Ervi. When I first started seeing Elke, she and a friend sometimes walked to my house. Once she called to make sure I was home, as she had to walk about a mile, and my father answered the phone. She asked if Ervi was home and my father turned to my mother and said, "Someone is asking for Ervi. Do you know an Ervi?"

My mother laughed and told him, "Heshy is Ervi." He had no idea. To this day, all my friends call me Ervi, but everyone in my family calls me Heshy. I was named Ervi because they needed a secular name on the birth certificate; my aunt Regine was reading a book whose main character's name was Ervi. At some point, I hated everyone questioning my name and the spelling, so I started saying my name was Irving, which was much more common. I registered for the draft as Irving, which later caused problems with the IRS when I reverted to Ervi, which I liked by then because of its uniqueness.

At the school I was now in, the Hebrew and English studies were more rigorous than in any of my previous yeshivas. The more Orthodox the yeshiva, the less emphasis on the English subjects. In all of my yeshivas the Bible, or Talmud, was translated from Aramaic to Yiddish. Everyone in the schools spoke Yiddish, and most of the students' parents were Holocaust survivors from Eastern Europe. Thus, I grew up thinking all Jews had been directly touched by the Holocaust. Almost all of my friends' parents also spoke with accents.

The difference at Yeshiva Toras Emes was that most of the students were Modern Orthodox and very few had *payes* (sidelocks), although many did at the other yeshivas I had attended. My friends in Toras Emes, being Modern Orthodox, were interested in sports and collecting baseball cards, both of which I loved. I never really had enough friends near my house to play sports or trade cards with, but at school I did. At lunch, we played punchball on the street in front of the school. On weekends, we played stickball in the playground.

I was a good student and enjoyed my years at Toras Emes. At the end of sixth grade, I was one of three students asked to complete some seventh-grade math workbooks and told that ,if we did well, we would skip seventh grade—which is exactly what happened. I went directly into eighth grade and made some new friends but, for the most part, hung out with my former grade.

I also went to Yankee Stadium several times with my friends. My parents, as I noted, didn't understand or follow any American sports. But that did not discourage me from becoming an avid fan. My friends and I rode the subway from Brooklyn to the Bronx, and I recall how awed I was the first time I entered Yankee Stadium from the right-field gate. I was used to playing softball on concrete fields in the parks near my house, and suddenly I was watching players taking batting practice and shagging fly balls on something that was huge and green and manicured. It was incredible. We brought our own sandwiches because we only ate kosher food. Watching Mickey Mantle, Yogi Berra, Whitey Ford, Roger Maris and the rest of those great Yankees was like seeing the black-and-white pictures on my wall come to life in technicolor. Those were the great years with Maris and Mantle chasing Babe Ruth's record of 60 homers in a season and with the Yankees winning several World Series. Maris broke Ruth's record with his 61st homer on the last day of the 1961 season, although just about everybody wanted Mickey to break the record, since he was a bigger star than Maris and had been a Yankee for a lot longer. But Mantle got hurt toward the end of the season, leaving Maris to pursue Ruth's record by himself.

In any case, it was a great time to be a Yankee fan. When Sue and I had Elissa and Eric, I made sure to go as a family to baseball and basketball games. Sometimes, it was just Eric and I who went to Knicks games, or to visit spring training sites, sharing our love of sports. Sometimes all four of us went to baseball or basketball games together. Alternatively, Elissa made me her "Reese buddy" since we went to several Reese Witherspoon movies together. I still enjoy thinking about those times, perhaps because I didn't get to do that with my own parents.

My father, meanwhile, still worked at Goodstein Bros. but he also started making and selling suits, sports jackets, slacks and coats from our apartment. People would come and get fitted, choose the material, and then my father would make the garment. I would also go to various places in the Garment Center to pick up suits or coats to bring to my father, which he would then alter. It was a fairly quick ride on the Sea Beach line. They knew me as Willy's son and always had the package waiting. I usually went on a Friday because we had a half day of school on that day.

As time went by, my father's business at home seemed to be going pretty well. He always had several suits or other garments hanging in the hallway closet or on hooks in the foyer area. His dream was to eventually leave Goodstein Bros. and have his own business and do what he loved while working for himself. He took pride in his work and had repeat customers, as well as other customers who came through word of mouth. I learned through his example to take pride in what I did and go the extra mile. Years later, when I started my own private practice as a psychologist, I saw this pay off as well. Patients would return when new issues arose and others came via word-of-mouth referrals. In treating all my patients with respect and care, they could tell I took pride in what I did and it encouraged them to also give their best efforts in the therapeutic process.

Writing about those trips to pick up clothing for my father reminds me of the famous New York City blackout on November 9, 1965. I was 15 and on the train on my way home. Around 5:00 p.m. the train suddenly stopped. We were in the tunnel between the Brooklyn Bridge and the DeKalb Avenue station. When the train halted, everyone was calm because we thought it would be a short wait until the trains in front of us left the station and we started moving. However, our train remained stuck—and then the lights in the train went out. In the end, we waited almost four hours in the train until someone came along and told us all to walk to the front car. From there, we walked out the subway door onto the catwalk along the train tracks. I was carrying a large package from the Garment Center, and there was an elderly lady in front of me who was having difficulty walking on the catwalk, which was very narrow. I helped her by carrying both her package and mine. When we finally got to the DeKalb Avenue station, we learned there was a blackout in the city and no trains or buses were operating. There were huge lines at the phone booths, so I couldn't make a phone call to have my father pick me up by car. I decided I was going to walk home, which was at least six miles from where I was stranded. However, the lady whom I had assisted hailed a taxi, saw me and asked me where I was going. She told me she could drop me off at 65th Street and 5th Avenue, and from there I could walk to 69th Street and 21st Avenue. Which is what I did. I was saved from walking at least three or more miles of my long journey home because the woman I helped on the catwalk wanted to return the favor. I did end up walking the rest of the way after the taxi dropped me off; when I got home, our building, for some reason, still had power. Every other apartment building or house I walked by was pitch black. What was also amazing to me was how calm my parents were when I finally walked in the door. They knew about the blackout and somehow, despite the fact I was over six hours late and had walked over three miles in the dark, they were pretty relaxed about the situation. I was really surprised, but my father told me he knew I would figure out a way to get home. I didn't get it at the time, but it is something I want my children and grandchildren to know: You have what it takes and no matter what you have to deal with, you will figure things out and get where you need to be, even if it's not that easy.

Two additions to the family occurred during our time in Bensonhurst. At the end of 1958, Uncle Moishe went to Metz (in France) to see my grandfather and also to meet his future wife, Rosette Rosenfeld. Rosette's mother's aunt was related to my grandfather's wife, Tante Fella. They were introduced and apparently, he fell in love and they married in France on December 9, 1958. They came to live in Jackson Heights in Queens for several years. Rosette worked as a beautician and Moishe continued working as a solderer at Momo Corporation. As a couple, they were great friends with his friends, Alex and Jack from Sweden, and their wives. They all skied and went bowling together and enjoyed one another's company. Rosette became a citizen but a few years later, she and Uncle Moishe moved to Metz. Rosette's father and my grandfather helped set up Uncle Moishe to run a clothing store, and he and Rosette worked in the store together for several years before they had two children, Babette and Dany. Her father, Charles, and Moishe got along quite well, and they had plenty of opportunity to spend time together, as Charles' store was on the same block as Moishe's store. Tante Fella would be instrumental in finding a wife for my uncle Victor as well about 15 years later.

On July 8, 1961, my sister, Brenda was born. My parents had

always wanted a girl. She was named after my father's mother, Brana, who died in the Holocaust in Auschwitz. Babette, Uncle Moishe's daughter, was also named after her. Brenda's middle name, Pamela, was after my father and mother's grandmother, Pava. Her Hebrew name is Brana Pava. My parents were thrilled to have a girl, and she was fawned over. She initially slept in my parents' bedroom, and then she was moved into the bedroom with Eddie and me. She was 11 years younger than me and 7 years younger than Eddie. I can recall times we all went to the grocery store (there were not that many supermarkets yet) down the block from our apartment; when we got there, my mother would put Brenda's carriage in front of the store, and we would go in and buy the things we needed and then come and get Brenda in the carriage and go home or do other errands. (Everyone did this in those days. If someone left their child unattended now, the police would be called, along with Child Protective Services.) Those little grocery stores seemed to have everything, even in a fairly small space. Of course, you had to go to the butcher to get your meat, to the fish store to get your fish and the bakery to get baked goods and bread. I hated passing the fish store because I couldn't stand the smell of it. Even now, the smell bothers me.

All this while, my father's business was growing and he had to install racks on the ceiling in our bedroom to hold the amount of clothing he bought. I had a rack of suits above my bed, Eddie had sport jackets above his and Brenda had a row of slacks above hers. At the time, we did not think it was weird because everyone we knew, including Uncle Benny and other friends who were tailors, was working out of their homes as well. As I think back on it, yes, it was a little strange. Benny, after all, had much more room in his house in Canarsie, where the clothes were on racks in his basement.

Eventually, in the early 1960s, things changed. My father bought a store on Woodhaven Boulevard in Rego Park, Queens. He named it Willhaven Cleaners and Tailors. It was a dry cleaning store but the primary earnings were from the tailoring and alterations he and his other tailors did. He always had another tailor working with him. He brought most of his inventory to the store but he continued to work out of the apartment until we moved into a house in Kew Garden Hills in Queens in the summer of 1967.

As it turned out, my father's store was in a non-Jewish neighborhood, and stores were closed on Sundays. He started opening the store on Saturdays to accommodate the people who could only come in on the weekend. By then, I was working in the *shul*, leading the junior congregation every Shabbos for $25.00 a week. When I was asked where my father was, I told the adult congregants that he went to the early *minyan* elsewhere, which is what he asked me to say. This created a huge internal dilemma for me, which I did not realize at the time but learned years later when I was in therapy during graduate school.

Over the years, I have told my friends stories about how, for several years while growing up, my family lived with racks of clothes over our beds. I can honestly say, I never gave it a second thought as a kid. I also realized as a kid that we were not rich. I had very few toys and games, and never owned a new baseball glove or bicycle while growing up. I learned how to ride a bike when I was 10 or 11 years old when we visited family friends—Simon and Rita from Liege—in Detroit one summer. They had a son named Harry, who was my age, and a daughter named Sonya, who was Eddie's age. They both had bikes, and I learned to ride on Sonya's bike after bruising myself pretty good from falling on the bar that ran across Harry's bike.

When we got home from Detroit, I of course wanted a bike and got a used one from our next-door neighbor, Julie Kliegerman, a widow who worked in the city. It was actually Julie's nephew, who was about to go off to college, who passed down his used bike to me. I spray-painted it an ugly green color to hide the rust, but no matter how it looked, I loved this bike as it enabled me to ride all over Brooklyn to see my friends and to explore different neighborhoods. Julie also gave me her nephew's left-handed glove, which I had to figure out how to use because I was right-handed. I appreciated, took pride in and loved whatever I had. It did not matter that it was used; it was mine. I was also used to getting some hand-me-down clothes from family friends.

When I turned 13 and started working, I was expected to buy my own clothes—beyond the two pairs of pants and shirts I got from my parents for the new school year. I learned the value of money and the need to make choices about how to spend it. I guess, if you don't have much, you appreciate what you do have. In many ways, it seemed we had a great deal because I never felt we lacked for anything. That influenced how Sue and I came to the decision to give our children an allowance to learn how to make choices regarding the things they wanted. Prior to giving them an allowance, no matter what store we went into, Elissa and Eric always wanted something. Once we gave them an allowance and they would ask to buy something, we would say, "You have some money, and you can spend it on this or save it to buy something you really want." All of a sudden, they started looking at prices and deciding if a particular thing was as necessary as they initially thought it was. It also informed our decision to have Elissa and Eric work after school during high school and in the summers. Of course, we bought them lots of things throughout their childhood, paid for their colleges and summer camps and so on—we were not expecting them to rely on their allowance all the time. That would not have been realistic. In any case, I believe our approach paid off because they are very good with money and have never asked us for any since moving out after college.

While we were still living in Bensonhurst and I was getting older, I traveled to my friends by bike or by foot. As I previously noted, many of my friends lived in either Borough Park, which was a two-mile walk, or over a mile away near the Bay. Twice I recall walking home, after visiting friends, when several kids came up, surrounded me, took my yarmulke off my head and punched me—and then ran away. It was my first experience with anti-Semitism, which I believe these kids had learned from their parents. In those days, Bensonhurst was made up mostly of Italians, Germans and Jews, and where we lived was heavily Jewish. Still, as you walked, you would come to neighborhoods that had very few, if any, Jews living there, and that's where trouble could arise.

I was a good student and took a test to see if I would be accepted at Yeshiva University High School of Brooklyn. It was also called Brooklyn Talmudical Academy (BTA) and was located on Church Avenue near Erasmus Hall High School in Flatbush. It was an elite school and only took in about 50–55 students per grade. I was accepted into the school and was proud of getting in. I loved being there and made some great friends. Since the classes were small, everybody knew one another, and I joined the school newspaper and wrote about the BTA basketball team, which was called the Yugers. But it turned out that writing for the newspaper and playing basketball were the only things into which I really put any effort. I would go in early, telling my parents I was going to go to the morning-prayers *minyan*, but instead played basketball in the schoolyard with some friends. I put almost no effort into schoolwork, which was totally unlike me. I also hated the rabbi who was my teacher for two years in the morning classes. He was a miserable human being who had favorites and said mean things to students who weren't a part of that group.

I realized early on that being a rabbi did not necessarily make you a good person. Being a rabbi was a job often filled by good people but sometimes by people who had no business in that role. Years later, I would have a second revelation when I worked at St. Martin of Tours Catholic School and saw a nun bullying students and disciplining them by hitting them with a ruler. While almost all the nuns in the school were nice people, observing how this one nun acted was very shocking to me. Perhaps I was surprised because it was a woman dressed in a nun's habit. In any case, it simply reaffirmed how the job does not make the person, and that it is much more the other way around.

As for my schoolwork, after two years of lackadaisical effort, the principal called my father and asked him to come in for a meeting. He basically told my father I was not the kind of student who usually represented the school. The school prided itself on the number of students who received Regents Scholarships and they didn't think I would help their statistics. In other words, I was being expelled. My father asked if they would give me another chance and that he would pay more in tuition, but they refused to reconsider. My father was furious with me and didn't talk to me for several days. I was embarrassed about what the principal told him, in addition to the fact I was getting thrown out of school. I told my father I didn't want to go to another yeshiva. Instead, I enrolled in the local public high school, Lafayette High. I couldn't believe how easy the school was. I did very well and was home by 2:00 p.m.

every day. School was a piece of cake as far as I was concerned—and I could play basketball at the park and still have plenty of time to do my homework. At Yeshiva University High School, I didn't get home until 6:00 to 6:30 in the evening and then had homework, which, of course, I wasn't doing.

My father, meanwhile, insisted I go study with a rabbi in a seminary near our apartment. I loved the rabbi and he was a true Torah scholar with incredible wisdom. I did well and enjoyed the several months I studied with him—and then I just stopped going. There was no real reason for discontinuing my studies with him, but I just chose not to go.

I believe my being in a bible study group the past 30 years is due in large part to this rabbi and perhaps some of the better rabbis I had as teachers in the various yeshivas I attended. The rabbi I studied with for several months said several things that stayed with me. He identified with the Torah and Judaism's ethical philosophy of "compassion that leads to action." Being a good Jew is about doing, not just praying. It is about mitzvahs, such as charity, visiting the sick, helping those who need help, and so on. In the end, it is about being a *mensch*, a good person. He also said that studying Torah was a lifelong task. The goal was not to figure it out; there is always more you can learn. Studying was an ongoing process to see how we might better understand as we grew and evolved. He encouraged asking questions and having doubts, as opposed to many other rabbis I had as teachers who made questioning seem sacrilegious.

My grandfather was a Torah scholar his whole life. As we get older and perhaps, wiser, we see things and understand things differently. That is why you can go over something in the Torah you studied before and understand it differently later in life. I am a true believer that life is about constantly learning and improving yourself.

Years later, in therapy, my therapist helped me realize my behavior leading to getting expelled from Yeshiva University High School was an unconscious rebellion. I was rebelling against Judaism and everything I had been taught in yeshiva. Subconsciously, I was choosing my father over the religious tenets I had been indoctrinated in throughout my yeshiva years, as well as within my own family. I was deciding that it was acceptable for my father to work on Shabbos. When I finally had this revelation, I decided not to share my insights with him because it would only have hurt him to think he had in some way been responsible for my behavior in high school. I realized he was doing his best to take care of his family and that meant working on Saturday. I also realized how much I loved my father when I chose him over religion, God and everything I had been taught to believe at that point in my life. I must admit, I have moved away from Orthodox Judaism. There is still comfort in its traditions and its ways of praying and learning and the values that it teaches. However, I am clear that my values really come from my parents and the way they behaved by being so loving, warm and welcoming. From them, I learned I needed to be a role model for my children and grandchildren in the way I act on a daily basis. I have always said that the most important job one has is to be a role model to his or her children. I know I have helped many in my work as a teacher, school psychologist, psychotherapist, college instructor and supervisor of interns. What I am most proud of is how our children became the loving, warm and successful people they are, and that the spouses they chose to spend their lives with have the same attributes. They are all wonderful parents and role models to their children and our grandchildren. I couldn't be prouder of all of them. This *"menschlichkeit"* (which is Yiddish for the moral and honorable qualities in a person of good character) goes back to my parents and the generations who came before them. Family was always of utmost importance. Although my father worked on Shabbos, in the spiritual sense he lived a life of meaning, purpose and direction in relation to a higher power. And it is from my parents that I learned to live meaningfully and for a higher purpose. The Hebrew word for spirit is *"ruach,"* which literally means "breath." To me, spirituality means giving breath and hope to others. It is the underpinning of all that I do.

As I am writing this, two thoughts and lessons come to mind about my father's store. First, I worked with him in the store once I was in high school, to the point where I ran the store for the week or two in the summer when he took off to stay with my mother, Eddie and Brenda in the bungalow colony. I traveled from Bensonhurst by train and bus to open the store at 7:30 a.m. and close at 6:30 p.m. The tailor was there to do fittings, and I took in all the clothes to be cleaned and sorted the outgoing and incoming cleaning. It wasn't hard, but it was a long day. I realized the store owned my father more than he owned the store. I thus concluded it was better when he worked out of the house. He may have worked as many hours but he was able to be off on Shabbos and take at least two weeks of vacation every year. In the end, in 1987, he gave up the store and again worked out of the house in the basement. It enabled him to go to *shul* twice a day, eat lunch with my mother and grandmother and still do the work needed to make a living. Observing all of this, I promised myself I would never work on weekends and that family time would be a major consideration in whatever I eventually chose to do.

The second thing I think about was how my father interacted

with people who came into the store, especially Mr. Mendelson. Mr. Mendelson was retired and in his 80s and wanted to keep busy and involved. He told how he had been a milk-and-egg man who drove a wagon and made deliveries on the Lower East Side. He would come to the store when my father opened in the morning and my father would find various jobs for him to do—sweeping, putting hangers together and even making local deliveries. He worked slowly, but my father never said a word and would give him a few dollars for his efforts. He would have worked for free but more importantly he was engaged and felt he was doing something useful.

I also recall many people dropping in just to schmooze with my father. When that happened, he never stopped working. But he still managed to have conversations with them and seemed to enjoy the visits. One of those people was Sue's uncle Herman. The visitors lingered for quite a while, even though they had no dry cleaning or alterations that needed to be done. It may have helped that my father spoke several languages; but one time an elderly Chinese man came and spoke in Chinese, and I could see them seemingly engaged in conversation. Afterward, I asked my father how he had come to understand Chinese. He said, "I don't speak Chinese. He spoke Chinese, and I spoke Yiddish and we spoke."

Some of my earliest memories are of my parents respecting and befriending the elderly. In our building in Bensonhurst, we were always checking in on Mr. and Mrs. Lerman, Mr. and Mrs. Levine and Julie, whom Brenda referred to as Aunt Julie. Julie also dropped off the *New York Post* afternoon edition to me when she got home from work at 6:00 p.m. They were all significantly older than my parents but they were an extended part of our family. Respect for the elderly, making sure they were cared for, was ingrained in me—as was the belief that, if somebody comes in to talk to you, you make the time for them. I have even done this with potential patients I know I cannot see who call for an appointment. I always call back and try to find out the issue, so I can recommend the right therapists. After I give them a few minutes and take an interest, they usually ask if there is any way I can work with them. Sometimes they prefer to wait until I have an opening.

Giving people time to say what they need to may not always mean that much to you, but it often means a lot to them. I cannot tell you how many times somebody has told me how much I affected them by something I said to them when I can't even recall what I said. The important thing was that I gave them an ear, a little bit of my time and some respect and, in return, they felt listened to and cared for.

When I started at Lafayette High in my junior year, I met Henry Fink, who would become my best friend and, later, my roommate. Henry had just moved to Bensonhurst and was a cousin of a girl I was friendly with when I hung out at the Bay. We would meet at his apartment building, which was on the way to school, every morning. We were teammates on one of the two basketball teams I played on the last two years of high school. We worked as waiters in the Catskills together for several years and then, after college, shared an apartment. We also worked together at Yankee Leather Goods, a company owned by the father of one of our friends, Michael Ostrower.

Unfortunately, several years later, Henry became addicted to drugs and, during a summer trip to Afghanistan, was arrested on his flight back to the United States because he concealed hashish in his sleeping bag. Our friends were all at the airport, waiting for him, but he never showed up. I contacted Elizabeth Holtzman, who was representing our Brooklyn district in Congress. She found out that he had been arrested, and through her, we sent money (I personally sent $1,800.00) for his trial there. After that, I didn't hear from him for many years. When I finally did, he asked me to co-sign a loan, which I might have done if I hadn't been married and didn't have a child.

That was the end of our relationship. I realized he had never gotten in touch to tell me he was out of jail or to acknowledge the money our friends and I had sent him. He had drastically changed. He told me he had been let out of the Afghani jail because someone had started a fire near the bench where he slept and he had suffered smoke poisoning. The Afghans did not want an American citizen to die in their jail so they put him out on the street. He nursed his way back to health and eventually moved to Australia, where he traded jewelry and drugs.

Interestingly enough, Henry, Sue and I went to visit my parents when he returned to the United States, as they loved him. After our visit, my father said that Henry had changed and was not going to be who he once was. I am not sure what my father saw, but he knew, without any doubt whatsoever, that what Henry had gone through in Afghanistan had changed him forever. Unfortunately, he was right; after that visit, Henry returned to Australia, and we never spoke or saw each other again.

7

THE HOUSE IN QUEENS (1967–2018)

IN THE SUMMER OF 1967, MY PARENTS BOUGHT a house in Kew Garden Hills. It cost $22,000.00, and my father borrowed $1,000.00 from me and $1,000.00 from a family friend (Zisha) for the down payment. My father didn't have the cash because he was putting all his money into getting more inventory for the store. I was home that summer, so I knew about the move, but neither Eddie nor Brenda was told. It seemed to happen quickly, as I recall. The house was around the corner from Joe and Gilda Spiegel's house. I knew them from the bungalow colony, and my father knew Joe from being together in Sweden after the war. Both had been in concentration camps. Joe was my father's best friend until his death in the early part of this century.

Whenever my father spoke about Joe after his passing, he would well up with tears and talk about how much of a friend he was. He thought of Joe, not only as a friend, but also as a big brother. Joe used to tell me that my grandfather had once asked Joe to look after my father, and if he needed to, he could give him a "*potch*" (smack). Both of them would laugh at this story.

During my college years, Joe came to watch TV with us almost every night. Due to the fact I was going to college locally, I had my own room. It was small but big enough to hold a stereo/TV set. Eddie and Brenda had a much larger bedroom, which they shared. My parents had the other bedroom. On the first floor were the living room, dining room and eat-in kitchen. The basement was my father's work space and we watched TV together there as a family. It was also where Joe would join us.

Once in our new home, we immediately joined the *shul*, Torah Emes, a few blocks away and I went to *shul* every Shabbos. My father still had the store, so I went alone or sometimes with Eddie. I made friends there with a bunch of kids my age who were also starting college that year. Several of them were going to Yeshiva University and kept me informed about my friends from BTA, who were also attending Yeshiva.

The primary thing about moving to Queens was that my mother finally had the house she had always dreamed of. It reminded her of the house in Vilyatana, even though this one had two floors and a finished basement, unlike her single-story home there.

My father was somewhat concerned about the financial burden of buying a house, but my mother wanted this. It took years until she fully decorated it the way she wanted; she often bought a single piece of furniture, like a couch, and then a year or two later added a coffee table. While it took years to furnish all the rooms, it eventually became exactly what she wanted and everything matched. She was so proud of our home. I also recall my father taking care of his 4-by-10-foot garden in the backyard. In that small space, he grew, among other things, tomatoes, cucumbers, peppers, mint, zucchinis, eggplant and grapes. He tended that little garden throughout the year. In the winter he would pour coffee grounds and other leftovers for compost over the snow to help the garden grow in the summer months. For both of my parents, it must have been a reminder of the way life was once like in Czechoslovakia, where they had land and animals.

College

Since I had no idea that we were moving to Queens when I applied to colleges, I ended up at Long Island University in Brooklyn because my basketball friends from Lafayette were going there. LIU was a big basketball school, and they had several players who played there who ended up in the NBA and ABA. I eventually transferred to Queens College and graduated from there in 1971. I majored in history because that's what I loved to read about, and I especially loved reading biographies. The late Sixties and early Seventies were a time when our generation rebelled and pushed for change. I became more of a hippie/flower child than the yeshiva student I had once been. I joined sit-ins and marches to end the war in Vietnam. I loved the music of the era and began experimenting with various recreational drugs. I had always loved rock and roll, soul and blues, but now the music was evolving, becoming more psychedelic, the lyrics richer and capturing the feel of the emerging counter-culture.

I could feel my transformation from the naive, innocent "*yeshiva bocher*" (a student in a Talmudic academy) to someone who questioned everything. When Joe came over to watch TV, he would goad me into arguing about the war, civil rights, hippies, etc. It was friendly, and we enjoyed the give-and-take. I realized my parents weren't opposed to the way I viewed things because otherwise they would have argued with me or jumped in on Joe's behalf. They also saw that our country did not do right regarding civil rights, and they were also opposed to the Vietnam War: They had seen what war could make people do. As a result, I had a longer leash in my involvement in the sit-ins and in the culture change that was rampant on college campuses.

It was a very remarkable time because, had I gone to college a year or two before or after, I would not have experienced the Sixties in the same way. It was an incredible time of self-discovery by virtue of how young we were and what was taking place. Things aligned in such a way that I can't imagine I would be the same person had I not lived and experienced college during those years. In the end, I was influenced by it all. And I don't believe I could, or would, have gone as far away from Orthodox Judaism if it hadn't ben for those years during and after college.

Interestingly enough, I feel I am more spiritually Jewish now than ever before because I have actually questioned my faith and, having done so, resolved to have Judaism be an important part of my life. The things I have learned in adulthood have contributed to my spirituality, which was not the case when I attended yeshivas more out of obedience than choice. Most important, I have learned that it is the religious rituals and the tradition that bind us as Jews and I hope my children and grandchildren continue to enjoy and perform these rituals. When we perform them, we become one with all who preceded us and all who will follow. We are linked in a chain going back thousands of years. This collective connectedness can help to combat feelings of isolation, sadness and a lack of hope.

During my freshman year, Henry and I decided we would work

as busboys in a hotel in the Catskills because the tips were supposedly very good and it was undeclared income. We would be away from home, in the Catskills, with money to spend and plenty of people our age. So, one Sunday, we looked up some ads, and my parents drove us up to the Catskills, where we went from one hotel to another looking to get hired.

We did find jobs, and the hotel wanted us to come up for the week of Passover to see if we were capable of doing the work during the busy summer months. When we showed up the day before Passover, we were assigned to waiters, and each of us had three tables of eight people. We were told that breakfast was for several hours and guests came in to eat at any time during those hours. Lunch and dinner were at specific times, and all 24 people were served at the same time.

When the night of Passover came, Henry and I were told the waiters we were assigned to were not going to show up. Thus, we were going to wait and bus our own tables. We basically learned on the fly, but by the next day, we had it figured out and while we worked harder than those who had a waiter/ busboy team, we got the job done.

After Passover week ended, we basically told the owner we would only come back that summer if we were waiters and had our own busboys. He agreed, and the next two years we worked at the Ridge Mountain Hotel in Parksville. We did well financially and had a great time when we were off. We were close to the famous Grossinger's Hotel, which had a disco and lots of girls working there, and every other weekend, we went to a concert in a nearby hotel. I saw groups like Vanilla Fudge, Blood Sweat and Tears and Johnny Winter.

This was another example of doing a job for which we had no

experience but figuring it out as you went along. It was like my father's reaction when I finally found my way home from the New York City blackout. He knew I would figure out how to get home, and I did. In other words, don't be afraid.

During my junior year in college, a friend asked me what I would do after I graduated. I remember thinking that this was a good question and one I had given very little thought. I was a history major simply because I liked reading about history. I figured maybe I could teach it. However, because it was already my junior year, I did not have enough time to take the requisite 20 education credits (including student teaching for a year) before I graduated. I spoke to my professor in the Education Theory class, a man named Hal Sobel, who suggested I take as many credits as I could and then apply for a temporary per diem certificate. He told me if I got a job teaching history for one school year, I could get a permanent teaching certificate.

That is what I decided to do. Several years later, I ended up becoming friendly with Hal when I started teaching in the School Psychology program at Queens College, because we were both in the Education Department. I should note that neither of my parents graduated from high school—because of anti-Jewish laws my father stopped going to school around the time he would have been in sixth grade—and thus they had little idea how to help Eddie, Brenda and me with education issues, especially ones involving colleges. Yet, Eddie, Brenda and I ended up with master's and doctorate degrees. Education was important to my parents despite it being denied to them and even though Eddie, Brenda and I had to find our way by ourselves.

Around the same time, my maternal grandfather died in Liege. I remember my mother sitting *shiva* alone for her father. Uncle

Benny did not want my mother to tell Aunt Regine because she "wouldn't be able to handle it." As a result, my mother sat without her sister to mourn the loss of their father. Despite the loss of so many family members in the Holocaust, this was the first time either of my parents actually sat *shiva*. It was left to me to help my mother as she mourned because my father was working and Eddie and Brenda were in school. I had classes as well, but since Queens College was within walking distance, I was able to be present as people came to pay their respects.

Shortly afterwards, it was decided that my grandmother would come live with us. Uncle Victor and my grandfather had always taken care of her. Victor was now 30 years old, and my mother felt he needed to focus on himself. He was single, was in the army and, as a result, often had to be away from home for days or weeks at a time.

So my grandmother moved into our house in Queens. She was fine at first and seemed to adjust well. However, as time went on, there were episodes of paranoia in which she believed the Nazis were controlling the electricity and the water. She would go through periods of not touching the light switches or flushing the toilets and would mutter to herself about the Nazis who were everywhere, pretending to be neighbors or workers. When the medicines she was taking did their job, she was loving and always asking if we ate enough or wanted something to eat or drink. She would sit quietly and listen as she never learned to speak English. She spoke only Yiddish or French, preferring Yiddish.

I knew things were not good when she was quiet and not asking, in Yiddish, if I was hungry. She would just be in her head, staring or reading from her *siddur* (prayer book) or *tehillim* (psalms) and trying to quiet the noise in her head. As the years went by, there were several trips to hospitals for shock treatments.

Living with her, loving her and seeing how she was forever traumatized by the Holocaust only added to her impact on me. She was such a gentle and loving soul but she suffered due to her inability to put behind her the decision to hide her children in a convent/orphanage during the war. She could not appreciate how brave and wise she had been to have made that impossible choice. In fact, she was a "rescuer" who was unable to see herself in this role. By rescuing her own children and perhaps herself and my grandfather, she enabled all of them to survive. My grandmother also could not enjoy how resilient and successful her three children were and how they created good lives for themselves and their families despite those dangerous years hiding their Jewish identities in the convent/orphanage. Unfortunately, she never was able to stop running from the Nazis.

Europe and Israel (Summer 1971)

After graduating from Queens College, Henry and I, along with another friend named Kenny, decided to travel through Europe for the summer. This was an opportunity. not only to go abroad, but also to visit my grandfather ("Old Zeide." as my children called him), Uncle Moishe and Aunt Rosette in Metz, France, and my Uncle Victor in Liege, Belgium. Henry, Kenny and I each had a backpack and sleeping bag that attached to the bottom of the backpack. We landed in Amsterdam, and as we were going through customs, somebody came over to us and said he had several MDMA tabs (a kind of mood enhancer) but didn't want to go through customs with them, and asked if we wanted any. Henry and I took one each and swallowed it as we were going through customs. It's another example of risky behavior I would not recommend but was not unusual for those times.

We walked to the train station to go to Metz, and we were feeling good as we boarded the train for the two-and-one-half-hour trip. When we arrived, we walked to Uncle Moishe's apartment, which was only a few blocks from the station. He knew I was coming with two friends, and they'd set up a room for the three of us. We slept in Babette's room, and she slept in Dany's room with him. Since we got there late at night, they were already asleep. Babette was about 5 years old, and Dani was 2. Uncle Moishe and Aunt Rosette were up to greet us. She had prepared some food, which we ate as we all talked together.

After Aunt Rosette went to sleep, Uncle Moishe and the three of us stayed up most of the night talking and telling jokes. It was mostly Uncle Moishe telling jokes. This kind of joking and banter went on throughout the three days we were there. The fact that we looked like hippies did not seem to make one iota of an impression on them. I was their nephew, my friends were welcome in their home and that was that. We were fed like kings because Aunt Rosette was an exceptional cook. While we were visiting, they worked in their clothing store, and Aunt Rosette would leave the store at noon to stop and buy fresh fruit, vegetables and bread to prepare lunch and then dinner for all of us. Aunt Rosette could whip up various delicious dishes in minutes, and she served cold cuts and wine before lunch and dinner and cheeses afterwards.

Every night Uncle Moishe and Aunt Rosette took baths, and afterwards he would hang out with us and tell stories and jokes. We were laughing all the time. There was one joke he told about these three guys who always sat around telling jokes. They had so many jokes, they decided to number them so it would be faster to go through them. After they numbered the jokes, one guy would say, "24," and everybody would laugh. Another guy would say, "6," and everybody howled. The third guy said, "12," and nothing happened. This went on for another round, and when the third guy said, "26," ,again, nothing. So. the third guy asked, How come when the other two said a number everybody laughed but when he said a number, nobody laughed. The first guy said, "It's all in the delivery!"

We couldn't stop laughing. Afterwards, whenever we saw Uncle Moishe, one of us would say a number and he would crack up. After we left Metz, we'd send him a postcard from where we were with just a number on it. While in Metz, we also spent time with my grandfather. Henry and Kenny loved my family and couldn't believe how generous and welcoming they were.

From Metz, we took the train to Paris to pick up the rental car we were going to use for our travels. We rented a Renault, which had a stick-shift transmission. Kenny and I were going to be the drivers, as Henry did not have a license. Kenny had some experience driving a car with a stick shift, but this was going to be my first attempt. He gave me a quick lesson, and we decided I would drive so we could see if having a stick shift was a feasible plan. If not, we would have to trade it in for an automatic, which would cost twice as much. I pulled out into Paris traffic, and, of course, I stalled several times as I was driving around the numerous traffic circles, with other cars speeding past and honking at us. This went on for a while until, finally, I got the hang of shifting up and down without stalling and, especially, shifting into first gear after coming to a stop.

Later on during the trip, I had an accident in Athens and the three of us spent the night in a police car with two young officers who took us around the city, showing us various parks where they liked to hang out. It was more like a tour than an arrest. They held us because the accident had occurred at night and they needed proof we were insured. The next morning as we pulled into the police station with the officers, they already had confirmation we were insured. We also learned we would not have the car for almost a week, so we decided to fly to Israel, which was not originally part of the plan. For me, Israel was surreal in the sense everything I had learned and studied during my years in various yeshivas was now real and not just something I had read about. Seeing the Western Wall, Rachel's Tomb, Masada and the Dome of the Rock was incredible and made me almost glad to have had the car accident.

When we got back to Athens after six days, the car was ready. We then traveled through France, Holland and Belgium, where we stayed with Uncle Victor.

When we got to his apartment, we rang his bell and the landlady came out. I told her I was visiting my uncle, Victor Davidovic. She looked at us askance, rang up to him and in French said (as I later learned): "There are three long-haired men, and one of them claims to be your nephew." Victor reassured her I was, in fact, his nephew. He was hospitable as well and showed us around Liege. We also went to Germany, Italy, Austria and Yugoslavia. We had plenty of great times and adventures, including getting arrested in Rome for sleeping in a park in our sleeping bags because all the hostels were full. The police took our passport numbers and told us to leave Rome. We drove several miles out of Rome, parked the car on the side of a road somewhere and went to sleep in our sleeping bags. We were awakened by a dog barking two feet from us. The dog did not have a collar and looked vicious. Because we were so scared, we scurried into our car and slept there the rest of the night.

When we were in Munich, we traveled to Dachau to visit the concentration camp there. It was very intense to see the gas chambers and the ovens, as well as the barracks where my grandfather, father, and Uncle Moishe lived and managed to survive. It was horrifying to think about the family members who were murdered in these camps.

After we returned the car in Paris, Henry and Kenny wanted to spend the last three days in Metz with Uncle Moishe and his family rather than stay in Paris again. I was only too happy to get in touch with them to see if it was possible, and of course, it was. So that is what we did. "Family and friends are always welcome" is a Farkas family credo. From when I was a child to the day my parents died, visitors from Europe or from out of town stayed at my parents' home. For seders and any other occasions, my parents welcomed family and friends, even if it was just their children's friends. My mother always asked about our friends, and many of them talked about what great discussions they had with my mother.

Years later, when Elissa was 6 and Eric was about to turn 3, Sue and I visited Metz and stayed with Uncle Moishe and Aunt Rosette. We had such a great time with them that we, too, returned to spend more time with them at the end of our trip.

55 Ocean Avenue (1971–1974)

The last year of college and for a while afterwards, I worked at various mindless jobs at Yankee Leather Goods and Loeb Rhodes (a brokerage firm). That allowed me to make some money and be able to hang out with my friends and, I must admit, do a good deal of partying. I did a lot of stupid things that seemed O.K. at the time but looking back, were quite reckless. I always felt grounded, though, and never went to the extremes some of my friends did, including my roommate and best friend, Henry. I do not regret any of it because I believe it contributed to my understanding of those who go too far and/or make bad choices. It was at this time that a group of us went to Watkins Glen for a three-day festival with The Grateful Dead, The Band and the Allman Brothers. We camped there, and the tickets cost $10.00 for the weekend. The amazing thing was, we planned to meet some friends, Gene and Lisa, and somehow, despite the crowd of 600,000, we found one another.

My friends loved to listen to music, and several of them played guitar and would jam when we got together. At some point, I did not like being an audience member when my friends jammed and decided that I wanted to participate. So I bought a cheap guitar, learned how to play chords and within a relatively short amount of time, I was able to jam with them by playing rhythm while playing chords. We played rock and roll and 12-bar blues. I loved the few years I played and even wrote some songs and recorded them. Unfortunately, I can't find the tapes of these recordings.

I stopped playing at some point except when I got together with one of my best friends, Leigh Beekman, in California. Music and art were not something I was exposed to by my parents, nor in the yeshivas I attended. We did not have art or music classes. We didn't even have a gym. I feel I have some latent artistic talent that was not nurtured and perhaps some musical talent as well. As a result, I promised I would nurture creativity and the arts in my own children, and Sue and I did.

I had been going to Brooklyn every weekend for the four years of college because my friends were there. As soon as I graduated, Henry and I agreed we would look for an apartment together. We found a great place at 55 Ocean Avenue in Brooklyn. It was across the street from Prospect Park and a two-minute walk to the Botanical Gardens and the Prospect Park Zoo. We were on the third floor, overlooking the park. We each paid $100.00 a month for a huge two-bedroom apartment with an eat-in kitchen. We painted the living room lilac and the kitchen a shiny green, which seemed really cool at the time. My bed was two mattresses on the floor, and I had an antique dresser and a night table with a red light on it. Again, I considered these "furnishings" very cool. The most important room was the living room, which had the stereo system in it. We had a couch and a chair with no legs—we had taken the legs off so we could sit low to the ground. The hallway had multi-colored carpet mats that we put together. We also had two female cats that we named Mick and Keith because Henry loved Mick Jagger and I loved Keith Richards, and The Rolling Stones were our favorite band. Eventually, 55 Ocean became the hangout hub for our friends. Larry and Bonny Levoy lived on the first floor, and Michael Ostrower and Rick Tonis, and later Rick and Gene Goldman, and then Gene and Lisa lived on the fifth floor. Our other friends, Leigh and Shelly, and Bernard and Wendy, lived a mile or two away. It was a fun but crazy time. When Sue eventually saw the apartment, she was not as enamored as I was with the decor, to say the least. She thought I was "too freaky" for her. Somehow, I convinced her to not look at the packaging (long hair, scruffy clothing, etc.) but at what was inside. Luckily, she bought in.

Photo Gallery

My maternal grandfather, Efraim Davidovic, age 19, in Czechoslovakian army, circa 1925

My father, Wilhelm Farkas in cheder (first one to the left of the rabbi), age 8, circa 1937, Czechoslovakia

My mother, Esther, age 6, my maternal grandmother, Bruchela Davidovic, age 28, and Regine, age 2, circa 1935, Czechoslovakia

My paternal grandmother, Brana Farkas, née Sobel, and her sister, Hani, circa 1942, Czechoslovakia

My paternal grandfather, Samuel Farkas, circa 1942, working in the Carpathian Mountains (note yellow arm band), Czechoslovakia

My father lost five siblings in the Holocaust and four are shown here. From left: Chaim, Rivka, Ben Zion, and Deena Farkas who is lying on the grass, circa, 1943, Czechoslovakia.

My aunt Regine, age 8, and my mother, age 12, when they first entered convent/orphanage, 1942, Belgium

My mother and Regine at end of their second stay in the convent/orphanage, 1945, Belgium

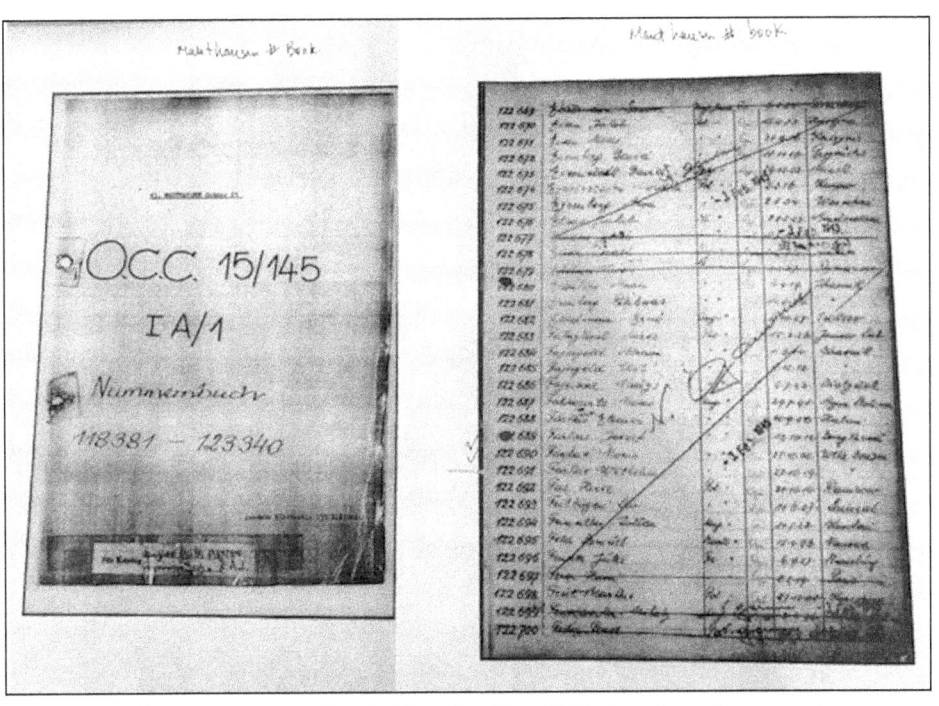

My grandfather's Concentration Camp prisoner card noting his move from Auschwitz to Buchenwald, June 6, 1944

Mauthausen Nummerbuch (Number Book) listing the prison numbers of my father, Wilhelm Farkas, and my uncle, Moritz Farkas

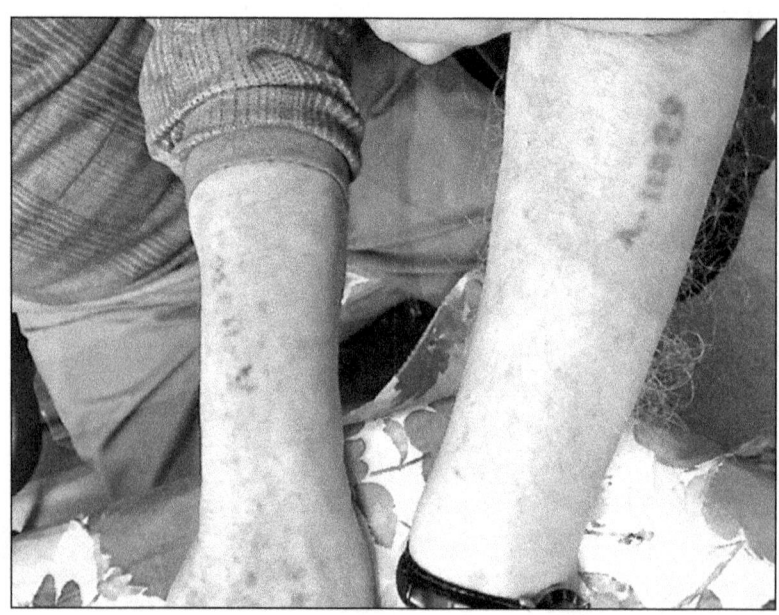

My father's International Red Cross Certificate of Incarceration, 1945. Note his KL Auschwitz number A-11030.

My father's arm with A-11030 tattooed on it and Uncle Moishe's arm with A-11029 tattooed on it

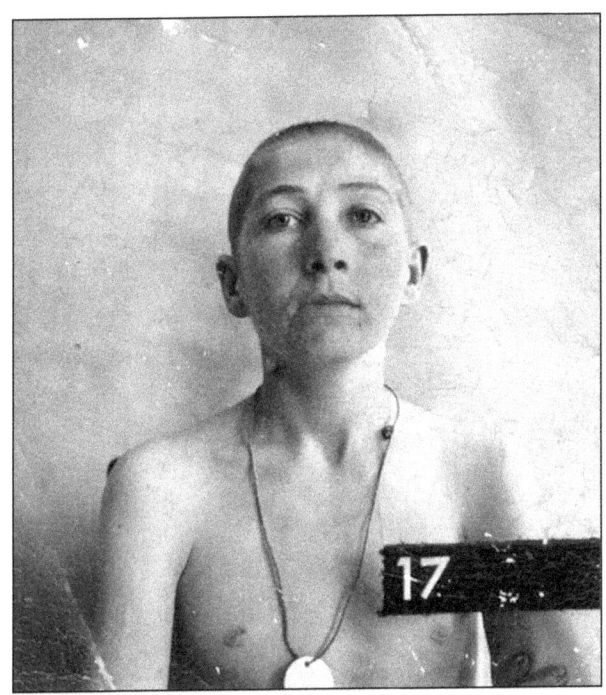

My father, Wilhelm Farkas, age 18, shortly after he was hospitalized following the liberation of the Bergen Belsen concentration camp, 1945.

Uncle Moishe, then 16 and my father, who was 19, in Sweden, circa, 1946

A party in Sweden, circa, 1948. My father is bottom left with a captain's hat. His best friend, Joe Spiegel, is on the far right, second row, sitting down.

My mother and father, in 1947, shortly after they first met in Belgium

My mother and father's wedding, January 5, 1949

My mother holding me, 1950

My father, me and my mother in the dining room aboard the SS United States on the way to New York from Belgium, November, 1952

The passenger manifest of SS United States. Our names are on the bottom.

Aunt Regine, Uncle Benny and me in Texas, 1953

Family gathering in Brooklyn. Standing from left: Tante Malchi, my mother, Mimi Olga, Aunt Regine, Uncle Avrum and my father. In front of them my cousins, Suri, Moishe Shmiel —and me, circa 1955

My brother, Eddie, my mother and me in the lake at our bungalow colony in the Catskills, New York, 1957

My maternal grandparents and Uncle Victor with my brother and me, 1958. The picture was taken in Liege, Belgium.

Uncle Moishe and Aunt Rosette's wedding in Metz, France, December, 1958

My grandfather, Samuel Farkas, Eddie, me, my mother, my father and Brenda at my bar mitzvah, March 1963

At Eddie's bar mitzvah in 1967. Bottom row, from left: cousins Morris and Suri, Mimi Olga, my mother and Brenda, Aunt Regine, Tante Malchi, Moishe Shmiel's wife. Standing from left: me, Eddie, Uncle Avrum, my father, Uncle Benny, Uncle Tzaler, cousins Moishe Shmiel and Ethel, 1967.

My father in front of his store, circa 1972

I was the best man at Aunt Suzie and Uncle Victor's wedding, in 1973. Pictured with me is Karen, Suzie's sister, the maid of honor and Suzie and Victor.

Family and friends at my parents' 25th wedding anniversary party in January 1974. From left: Joe Spiegel, Gutko Zimber, my grandmother (Babi), my mother, Chonek Zimber, my father, Gilda Spiegel and Uncle Benny. Aunt Regine is pictured in front of my mother.

Sue and me in the Grand Tetons, Summer 1975

Brenda, my mother and father, Sue and myself, my Babi and my Zeide, at our wedding in December 1974

Sue's mother and father, Frieda and Moritz Wertheim with Elissa, their first grandchild and our first child, in a picture taken in 1981

My father (holding Eric), me, and Sue's father at Eric's bris in 1984

Elissa, me, Eric and Sue in front of our house, 1985

My grandfather (Old Zeide) with Elissa after she sang at Brenda's wedding, 1987

Elissa with her Zeide, my father, in 1988

The Davidovic siblings with their mother (my maternal grandmother) in June 1977. From left: my mother, Babi, Aunt Regine, Uncle Victor

Our cousins from Belgium, the Sobel family. Bottom: Carole and Lisette Halpern (née Sobel) and top: Isy and Maximilian Halpern

Family picture at Elissa's bat mitzvah, February 1994. Standing from left: Victor and Melissa Davidovic; my father; my Babi; me; Sue's father, Moritz Wertheim; Sue; Marianna and Eddie Farkas; and Dan Bacharach, Brenda's husband. Sitting from left: my mother, Elissa, Eric (standing), Brenda, and Suzie Davidovic.

Family picture just before Eric's bar mitzvah, November 1997. From left: my mother and father, Elissa, Eric, me, Uncle Moishe, Cousin Dani, Aunt Rosette, Sue and Brenda.

My father at the Miami Holocaust Memorial Wall, pointing to the names of people in his family and Sue's family that were murdered during the Holocaust

My mother and father with their three grandchildren (from left) —Sammy, Eric and Elissa.

Eric kidding around with my father

Family members celebrating my parents' 60th wedding anniversary, January 2009. From left: Victor and Suzie Davidovic, Jer Neuman, my father, Mel Cwibecker, Morris Neuman, me and Ethel Cwiebecker.

Eric and Jess celebrate their wedding, May 5, 2012.

Elissa and Ben on their wedding day, December 19, 2015

From left: Me, Eddie and Brenda at Elissa and Ben's wedding, December 2015

A family picture at Elissa and Ben's wedding, December 2015. Back row from left: Melissa Pupelo, me, Victor and Suzie, Jer Neuman, Hymie Ingber, Eric, Sue, Brenda, Morris Neuman and Michael Pupelo. Front row from left: My father and mother, Aunt Regine, Jess and Sammy.

My mother realizing her goal to dance at Elissa and Ben's wedding. Top from left: My mother, Sue and me holding on to her walker as we start to dance. Below left: Elissa and my mother dancing after she discarded the walker. Below right: My mother dancing with Eric.

Our family from France on a visit to New York. From left: Aunt Rosette, Uncle Moishe, Cousin Babette, Sue, Cousin Dani (sitting), Eric and me.

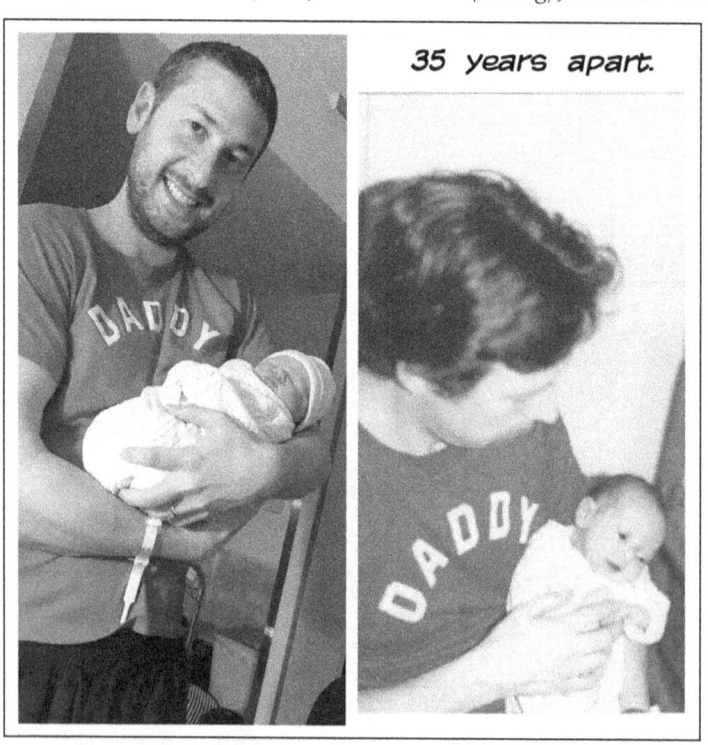

Eric holding Sienna, March 2016, while wearing a shirt I wore 35 years earlier when I held Elissa in March 1981.

My mother holding her first great-grandchild, Sienna, with Brenda and Sammy. Picture was taken in 2016

My mother holding her second great-grandchild, Zachary William Halperin, at his bris on October 24, 2017. He was named after my father.

From left, Eric, Jess, Elissa and Ben with Sue and me at Sammy's bar mitzvah, October 6, 2018

The next generation, October 2021: From left, Zoe, Sienna, Ruby, Zachy. Ruby Eve Farkas and Zoe Esther Halperin were named after my mother.

With our grandchildren in December 2021. From left: Sienna, Zachy, Zoe, Grammy (Sue), Zeide (myself) and Ruby.

8

LIFE WITH SUE

Adams School and Sue Wertheim

AT SOME POINT, I REALIZED I needed to look for a job as a history teacher. I went to the New York City Board of Education at 110 Livingston Street in Brooklyn. I was told that there was a glut of teachers, especially history teachers. It turns out that, during the Vietnam War, being in college or being a teacher enabled you to get a deferment. Thus, there were more teachers than needed. It was suggested I try to get a job in a private school.

I started looking at Brooklyn private schools that were listed in the phone book. One day I went to the Blueberry School; they told me they did not need teachers, but they said they had heard the Adams School in Manhattan was hiring. I looked up the school and decided I would go there first thing the next morning.

I got there early, went to the office and told them I was looking for a position as a history teacher as I had a temporary, per-diem secondary-school certificate to teach social studies. The secretary looked at me and told me the reading teacher had just called in sick and asked if I could teach reading. I said, "Sure." The truth is, I never took a reading class at Queens College but I figured I had never taught history, either, so I was willing to do it. I thought to myself, Let's do it, I'll figure it out. I must have channeled my father's daring, such as volunteering to work on electricity in the labor camps when he had no idea at all how to do so.

The secretary gave me the schedule, and I went to the class. The Adams School was housed next to a church and had small classrooms. As the students walked in, I realized there were around 10–12 in each class. When they sat down, I introduced myself and asked them what their teacher, Mrs. Adler, had done the previous day. One of them told me, and I suggested we do more of that. I repeated this the next few periods.

When the third-period class entered, some of the students looked developmentally challenged but were pretty well-behaved. When it was my lunch period, I went to the faculty room and introduced myself as the substitute for Marilyn Adler. I asked what kind of school the Adams School was. I can recall one of the teachers loudly laughing and saying, "We got a novice here." Nevertheless, I was told it was a special-education school (K–12) and the lower grade classes were housed in another building several blocks away.

In any case, I had taken on a real challenge. Not only had I never taken a reading class—I had never taken a special-education class either.

I made it through the day, and I was asked to sub for her the next two days as well. By the end of the week, I became the school's permanent sub, which was a great experience, as I was placed in classes from kindergarten through high school.

I made it basically on guts and instincts. I learned a great deal about working with children of different ages and in dealing with the different challenges the students had to confront. I became friendly with several teachers, including Sue Cowen, Miriam Smith and others who gave me some great ideas that I could use in the classroom.

After a month of being a substitute teacher, I was asked by Jack Eber, who was the director of the middle school, if I wanted to become a full-time teacher on the middle-school level. They were going to start a class with new entrants, as well as students in other classes, to make those classes easier. I said I would do it, but I would need one period of teaching high school American History so I could get my permanent teaching certification. He agreed, and that's how my career in education really began to take shape. My willingness to teach a reading class on a minute's notice and not flinching was the beginning point for my career. I was lucky I didn't have time to think for a few minutes that first day, or I might have begged off.

I loved working at the Adams School. I made it on my instincts and not being afraid to ask colleagues for lesson ideas. I was good at establishing relationships with the students, who were emotionally challenged and/or neurologically impaired. They were not successful in the public school system, so they were sent to schools like the Adams School. My students were mostly good kids who adopted tough-kid personas, so nobody would realize they had trouble learning. We established a great bond, and the kids named themselves "The Wild Bunch" and later the "Farkas Bunch." When they changed their collective name to the latter, they would sing the theme song to the *Brady Bunch* TV show, changing the words to the Farkas Bunch. They basically made us a family. I believe they did whatever I asked because they trusted me and knew I was there for them and not because I was a great teacher. I had a good idea to get them to write by starting a newspaper called the *Junior Level Post*. It worked, and everyone contributed, including one student who had trouble writing but was a good artist. Years later, I figured out why many of the things I did instinctively at the Adams School worked so well. I even wrote an article that was published about the *Junior Level Post* and how I got students to write for it.

I made some good friends at Adams and several became lifelong friends: Sue Cowen, Jack Eber, Joy and Harvey Simon (through Sue Cowen). And of course, the Adams School is where I met Sue.

Towards the end of the 1972–1973 school year, I was asked to be the best man at my Uncle Victor's wedding. Victor is my mother's younger brother. He was about 32 years old at the time and was in the Belgian army, where he had learned to be an engineer. He had met Susan (Suzy) Zimber in Metz, France, through my paternal grandfather and his third wife, Tante Fella, who was a relative of Suzy's. Suzy was living in Israel at the time and came to France for a wedding in August of 1970. It was arranged for her to meet Victor at this wedding. Suzy was smitten and knew she would eventually marry him. She went back to Israel, and he went back to Liege. They stayed in touch. Victor still had several years to serve in the army and was working with NATO forces in Germany. Finally, after several years, they became engaged and planned to marry on June 17, 1973, in Washington Heights.

Suzy's background was similar to my family's. She was born on

July 24, 1947, to Chunik and Gutka Zimber. Her parents had been in various concentration camps during the Holocaust. They had met and married after the war and were living in Hanover, Germany, when Suzy was born. The family eventually emigrated to Israel and then to the United States. They lived in Washington Heights and the Bronx, as well as several different areas of Brooklyn and even Detroit for a while. During her college years, Suzy traveled, made *aliyah* and moved back to Israel.

When I got to the wedding to put on my tuxedo, I was introduced to Suzy, her parents, her sister Karen and Karen's husband, Hal. Afterwards, I went out to join the other guests, and I saw Jack Eber, who was my supervisor at the Adams School. I asked him, "What are you doing here?" It turned out his family and Suzy's family, along with several other families, had known one another for years. The families had come from the same area in Poland and, after moving to the United States, gone to the same bungalow colony every summer and were all longtime friends.

I eventually learned that Suzy's father had met Jack's parents, Betty and Ruben Eber, after the war, and that they had lived together in Germany in the mid to late 1940s. They eventually lost touch, but in another interesting story, in 1959, serendipity reunited them. Suzy's parents were living in Brooklyn, and one day when her father was parking his car, he was blocked by a woman with a shopping cart. It was Betty Eber. When he realized it was Betty, he started honking his horn and yelled out, "*Betka!*" She started yelling back at him because he was honking his horn at her. Finally, she realized who it was and ran to him, and they hugged each other. After a short conversation, they realized they were living in the same apartment building. It turned out Jack had also been born in Germany in 1947, when his parents and Suzy's parents were displaced persons there. This is another example of how people came together and met in unexpected ways years after the war. Sue (whom you are about to meet) and I met many of the families in this group in the ensuing years through Suzy and Jack.

And now, finally, the story of how I met Sue Wertheim, the woman who would become my wife. She had started working as a science and math teacher during my second year at Adams. She worked in a room two or three doors down the hall from me but I never saw her because she came in and left later in the day than I did. Furthermore, she apparently never left her room once she arrived in her class.

One day in November 1973, we were at a teachers' meeting, trying to start a union, as we were grossly underpaid for what we did compared to teachers in New York City public schools. I was lying on the floor with my head resting on my backpack, listening to the teachers who were speaking, when this beautiful woman with long, dark brown hair parted in the middle walked into the room. I had never seen her before. I found out she taught on the high school level, and my American History students were in her math and/or science class. After the meeting, I introduced myself and asked about one of those students, just to make conversation.

Later, I was walking to the train with Sue Cowen and this same beautiful woman. She told me her name, Sue Wertheim. The next day, I walked into her class to ask for her phone number, and she gave it to me. I asked her out for Sunday night and we went to V&T, an Italian restaurant. We had a lovely dinner, and she told me she had friends who had just returned from India, where they had spent time with a guru. This would be her only chance to see them, and she asked if I would mind spending part of our date in a bigger group. I said it would be fine; we spent the rest of the evening schmoozing with her friends at a get-together. I then walked Sue to her apartment on 100th Street and West End Avenue. A few days later, I asked her out for the following Friday and, again, she agreed. When I got to her apartment, she opened the door and, shortly thereafter, began to cry. When I asked her why she was crying, she told me she just had an argument with one of her roommates, who was questioning her about going out with me and whether she was really sure that her relationship with her former boyfriend in Philadelphia was over.

I listened and was able to help her work through her feelings. In the end, she felt sure her previous relationship was finished. At that point, we decided to stay at her apartment and we watched the movie *In Cold Blood*, based on Truman Capote's chronicle of the vicious murders of a Kansas family. It wasn't the best choice of a movie for a romantic evening, but we had been playing it by ear ever since she opened the door that evening. I realized later that I loved how open and vulnerable she was. This was quite different from what I had grown up with. I had learned to keep things in and take care of them myself, and as our relationship developed, she would enable (sometimes force) me to deal with and get things out. By the end of the evening, as I was leaving, Sue kissed me passionately, and I knew right then better things were to come. Being a good listener had paid off.

Sue arranged the next date, and we went to eat at Famous on the Upper West Side and then saw a performance of *The Pajama Game* on Broadway. I'll never forget how incredible Sue looked that evening. At the end of the play, as we were leaving the theater, we met Gary Goldsmith and his girlfriend, Brenda, who were coming down the stairs (they would become our best friends, and we would see one another almost every weekend). Afterward, Sue and

I went to her apartment, and the rest is history.

I introduced Sue to my parents for the first time at their 25th wedding anniversary party. It was being held at the house of their best friends, Joe and Gilda Spiegel, just around the corner from where they lived.

Sue was welcomed warmly by my parents, and she got to meet all of their friends and family, who were very warm and friendly to Sue as well. As I previously noted, my parents, along with their friends, were always welcoming to anyone I brought home. Adding to their group of family and friends was a way to make up for all the family and friends they had lost in the Holocaust.

Within weeks, Sue was practically living with me in my apartment. She kept her apartment but was hardly ever there. When Sue's parents called her apartment looking to speak to her, her roommate, Dina, would call Sue at my place, so she could return their call. Finally, I told her I thought it was time to tell her parents she was living with me.

Sue reluctantly told them we were living together, and her father blamed his skyrocketing blood pressure on her. He told her he was not handling our arrangement well and asked us to go speak to their rabbi. We agreed, and Sue and I went to see Rabbi Jerome Fishman, who had presided at her temple when she was growing up. He had resigned as the rabbi of that congregation and was now a practicing social worker.

We spoke for a while, and he explained he wouldn't like it if his daughter moved in with her boyfriend but he believed in freedom of choice. He thought we were two well-adjusted adults who seemed to know what we were doing. While he did not give us his blessing, he apparently spoke to Sue's father. We were never told what they actually said to each other, but the issue seemingly disappeared and we never heard about it again.

Sue's parents were easy to get comfortable with. They were immigrants, just like most of the adults in my life at that time. They had come to the United States once they realized life in Germany for people who were Jews was becoming more and more ominous. Sue's dad, Moritz, was the third of seven siblings born to Hirsch and Bertha Wertheim (*née* Plaut). He was born on May 25, 1907, and was sent to Hanover to learn tailoring when he was a teenager. He and his younger sister, Jenny, were the last of the siblings to emigrate to the United States, in 1938. They were sponsored by their siblings as well as by Rabbi Moritz Speier. Moritz lived with his eldest sister, Gerta, and her husband, Albert Moses, and their children, Marty and Helen. Moritz's mother was also living in the apartment, which was in Washington Heights, an enclave for German-Jewish immigrants. Moritz enlisted in the United States Army in 1944, served overseas and would become a U.S. citizen while stationed in Italy. Through a fellow soldier in his unit, Willy Steinberger, he was introduced to Frieda Katz in 1948. Willy was Frieda's cousin.

Frieda Katz was born in Nentershausen, Germany, on November 26, 1912. Her parents, Soloman and Selma Katz (*née* Steinberger), had a house in Nentershausen. Frieda had two sisters, Irma and Edith, who were, respectively, two and four years younger than her. They had a good life in Germany until Adolf Hitler began enacting anti-Jewish laws. By 1935, patrons were boycotting Jewish-owned stores, and Soloman lost his butcher shop. They began discussing plans to emigrate to the United States as Selma had a half-brother, Jacob Steinberger, living there and he signed affidavits to sponsor them. Edith was the first to leave Germany for the United States in 1938. She then awaited the arrival of the rest of her immediate family as well as her future husband, Ludwig Reichenberg. Germany was still allowing Jews to emigrate then, and Frieda found out her papers were ready. She had to travel to Genoa, Italy, to embark on her voyage to the United States. It was an arduous trip as the ship, the *USS Washington*, barely escaped a German torpedo. The ship arrived safely in New York in 1940. Ludwig had already arrived, and he and Edith got married. Frieda, meanwhile, moved in with her aunt and uncle in Queens and took a job as a nanny on the Upper West Side of Manhattan, a job that she continued to do for the next eight years.

Unfortunately, Frieda's parents and her sister Irma never made it out of Germany. Years later, she found out they were murdered in Sobibor, an extermination camp built by the Nazis as part of Operation Reinhardt in Poland. This was part of the Final Solution to kill all of Poland's Jews. The loss of her parents and sister nagged at Frieda the rest of her life. She saved all of her correspondence with her family in Germany, and Sue has them to this day.

Moritz and Frieda married on Valentines Day 1948, after a year of dating. A little over a year later, on April 8, 1949, Susan was born. They were devoted to her, and she, in turn, adored them. When I met them towards the end of 1973, they were very welcoming, and I always felt comfortable in their presence. They met my parents and the rest of my family soon after, and they all got along very well. As my parents would say, they became family.

Meanwhile, I was enjoying teaching at the Adams School and enrolled in the Masters in Special Education program at Hunter College. Through my studies, I began to figure out why some of the techniques I used with my students worked well, and I also learned some new teaching skills. Interestingly enough, at the Adams School, it was the *students* who figured out "Farkas is going out with Wertheim," and they were rooting for us because they liked us both. At the beginning of the next school year, Sue and I both interviewed for jobs at the New York City Board of Education. Sue got a job teaching at Harambee Prep, where she was only a few years older than her students, some of whom had babies already. I got a job teaching at Ditmas Junior High School in Brooklyn. It was the first New York City public junior high school class for emotionally disturbed students in Brooklyn. There were two experimental classes, and I was teaching one of them. The students were generally not too difficult, although one of my students went to Macy's in the city in the morning and then came to school to sell what he had stolen. Another student had a sphincter-control problem and would frequently pass malodorous gas. The other students would run to the windows to open them up for air, and the student in question was always ready to punch out anyone who called him on it. I have many more stories from the students in that class, but the hardest part of teaching there wasn't the students. There were no books, and I had to make up practically everything without any support. By mid-year, I hated teaching at Ditmas and decided to look elsewhere for a job for the following year. Sue, on the other hand, loved the school where she was working. I was 18 credits into my masters program and only needed 12 more—four classes—to graduate with a masters degree in special education.

However, in 1975, New York City was on the verge of bankruptcy and was forced to lay off thousands of employees, including Sue and me. I saw this as a sign and decided to become a school psychologist. Before I started teaching at the Adams School, I had not known there were psychologists who worked in schools. At the Adams School I met two of them--Dr. Milt Kornrich and Steve Marburger—who were basically mentors to me. They had very different, but very effective, styles as school psychologists. When I was laid off, I resolved that that was the kind of work I wanted to do. I made the decision to apply to three schools—Queens College in New York City, UC at Hayward in California and Northeastern University in Boston. I was accepted into all of them, and Sue and I took a cross-country trip to visit friends in California, as well as to look at UC Hayward. Since Sue's parents were getting on in age and she was not ready to leave them, we decided to stay in New York and I would attend Queens College, where I had been an undergraduate. The best part of the program was the two-year internship. The first year, I interned three days a week at my old base, the Adams School, and learned so much that, when I then interned in Valley Stream's Howell Road School, it was relatively easy. My supervisor and principal at Howell Road School were surprised how knowledgeable I was and the way I could assess a student's difficulties and then implement an intervention plan. I also interned one day a week at Bedford-Stuyvesant Mental Health Clinic, which was an incredible learning experience. My supervisor there believed in phenomenological psychology, which I still employ to this day.

The term "phenomenological" refers to describing only what you see and not interpreting it. If you do ascribe something (for example, a feeling) to what you are seeing, you need to be aware that that's what you're doing. In addition, I took 12 credits of didactic instruction on Mondays plus one night a week. I had been accepted to the program with a proviso—I had to make up 24 undergraduate credits in psychology, because I hadn't taken these prerequisites as an undergraduate, except Intro to Psychology. Therefore, I had to attend Hunter College and Brooklyn College at night and, for one summer, Richmond College in Staten Island because it was the only program providing a class in experimental psychology. Thus, in two years, I completed 60 graduate credits in school psychology and 24 undergraduate credits in psychology for a total of 84 credits, all while interning three days a week the first year and four days a week the second. It just shows what one is capable of when the motivation is there.

If you had told me at any point prior to my getting laid off in 1975 that I would become a psychologist, I would have said you were crazy, as evidenced by my having taken only a single class in the subject during my undergraduate years. However, I believe I was meant to be a psychologist. I was able to seize the opportunity when I lost my teaching job. Before that, I was sure I would get my masters degree in special education and be a special-education teacher the rest of my working life.

And remember, my parents did not provide guidance regarding college or a career. It would be easy to say it was because they lacked educational opportunities due to the Holocaust, but I do not think it would have occurred to them to get involved even if they *had* had those opportunities. They were not guided by their own parents and had somehow figured it out. So they believed we would as well.

Thus, their three children essentially became successful in their professions on their own because of the belief that "you will figure it out." They believed in us, so we believed in ourselves. We just needed the opportunity to see what was out there. I often tell college graduates who have no idea what they want to do to just get out there and they will figure it out. The road of life has many forks, and you have to make choices along the way and cannot be afraid.

As a product of the Sixties, I thought we could change the world as we protested injustices and the Vietnam War. Then I realized we couldn't change the world.

I then thought that, if we couldn't change the world, at least I could change my little corner of it—my class, for instance, or the students and teachers I worked with.

Finally, I realized the only thing I could really change was myself. I realized if I did the best I could and strived to always learn more and be better, that was the most effective thing I could do. I also realized my becoming a teacher and then a psychologist emanated to some extent from thinking about what made people so hateful that they could do what the Nazis did. In addition, I also thought about what went into the makeup of other people who did not oppose what the Nazis did. I believe much hate comes from poor self-esteem and the need to blame or scapegoat others for what one feels is not right with oneself. The silence of others comes from fear and the sense one cannot impact the situation. Thus, I felt my goal was to be good at my job as a psychologist, treat everyone with respect, be authentic, listen and, most importantly, help others to feel good about themselves and aspire to become their best selves. In turn, they would then impact others by caring and listening and being *their* best authentic selves. In that way, there would be a ripple effect, since by being kinder to others they would feel good about themselves and behave kinder with others, and so on.

This is not accomplished in big "aha" moments but by continuously being all the above in interactions with others. I have had numerous people tell me how I impacted them at one time or another with something I said. I have found I often cannot recall the incident, as it wasn't something big or important to *me*, but it clearly meant a great deal to *them*. I try to be this way in all my interactions—with my patients, my students, my co-workers, my family or friends or somebody I pass in the street who may be asking for directions or nodding "hello."

Life is really an accumulation of many, many small moments. If we are lucky, we get a bunch of big ones, too. My views about acting out of love, being authentic and always trying your best was inspired by my parents and how they lived their lives.

Brooklyn: 1801 Ocean Avenue (1974–1978)

Sue and I got married several months after we started our jobs working for the New York City Board of Education. We also moved prior to that to 1801 Ocean Avenue in Brooklyn. It was several miles from our previous apartment at 55 Ocean Avenue. This one was a one-bedroom apartment with a pass-through kitchen window into the dining area. It was similar to the one on the *Mary Tyler Moore* TV show, which was a huge hit at the time. We thought it was so cool. I had a green thumb, so we had many plants throughout the living room area. It was "our" first apartment, unlike our previous one, which had really been my old apartment. We loved the apartment—until we were robbed in 1978. It was broken into, and our stereo, TV, cameras and jewelry were all stolen.

I always knew Sue and I would get married, and I sensed she felt the same. Unfortunately, I never proposed to her in a formal manner. This was not something any of my friends did at that time. I just felt great in her presence and realized she made everything more enjoyable. I tend to be low-key and, as my children say, "chill." Sue, on the other hand, feels things intensely and is totally into the moment. That is why any meal can be "the best" and any event "fantastic." Her enthusiasm and joy are wonderful to be around, and I probably do way more than I would if left to my own devices. We seem to balance each other out, and we love and enjoy each other tremendously. She makes me better. So, many years later, in a restaurant in front of our children and their spouses, I got down on one knee and formally proposed to Sue and presented her with the engagement ring she truly deserved.

Our wedding day—December 22, 1974—started out with beautiful, sunny weather. We weren't very involved in the planning. Although we had checked out the hall, the music was the only thing we really cared about.

The wedding was a gathering of three groups—Sue's parents' family and friends, my parents' family and friends and our friends. I can honestly say that they all had a great time. Sue was kind of shocked to see some of my Hasidic relatives for the first time. My grandfather, Uncle Moishe and Aunt Rosette came from Metz, and Uncle Victor came from Belgium. I shaved my beard to make Sue's father happy, but when I look at pictures of the wedding, I can't help but feel I should have kept it. My beard wasn't the only thing missing from the event. My brother, Eddie, had just left for Cali, Colombia, a few months earlier and didn't come back for the wedding. Our best friends, Leigh and Shelly, had just moved to Los Angeles because Leigh had enrolled in chiropractic college there and they were absent as well. In fact, some of the rest of the gang from 55 Ocean had also moved to the West Coast and weren't at our wedding, including Jerry and Randi Marder, and Rick Tonis. Despite missing my brother and some of our best friends, we had a really memorable time. On the way home from the wedding, it started snowing and it looked beautiful.

Jack Eber and Sue Cowen drove us home and we asked to stop the car near a house with incredible Christmas lights and decorations. And then, Sue, in her wedding gown, and I, in my tux, walked in the snow amid the lights and decorations. It created an image in my mind that to this day still seems magical.

Getting married was awesome, and we were excited to be Mr. and Mrs. Farkas. I was married to the woman whom I loved dearly and who made me feel complete. Jack painted a large, beautiful, abstract painting with a heart as the cornerstone as our wedding gift, which is still hanging in our home. We used some of the wedding money to buy our first car, a powder-blue Plymouth Duster. The air conditioner in that car never drained the excess water—there were times we drove it and it felt like a tank of water was swishing around every time we made a turn. Periodically we had to go to the garage next to our apartment building to have the water drained. Our first trip in the car was to get an egg cream in Sheepshead Bay and a slice of pizza on Kings Highway. It was our car, and we no longer had to borrow my parents'. I remember feeling this kind of pride about a car when my dad showed up one Friday at the bungalow colony with a metallic green Chrysler New Yorker. It was 1959, and the car was from 1954 but it was ours. We no longer had to be driven by others. I can recall taking a picture with my father in front of the car when I first saw it.

Now, we had a car, too. Sue and I drove the Duster cross-country later that summer. It was my first time seeing the country anywhere west of Detroit. The U.S.A. is so beautiful, and the natural wonders in the national parks are extraordinary. We loved it, as we mostly camped out and stayed with friends, especially in California. We have always valued our friends and would travel to see them often. Our children grew up with Leigh Beekman and his family, and Sue Cowen, even though they were 3,000 miles away. For me, this was a lesson learned from my parents, who traveled to Europe and other places to see family and friends. We would travel with Elissa and Eric cross-country many years later, and again it was grand.

During my second year in the Queens College program, Sue was accepted into the social work programs at Columbia University and Hunter College. She chose Hunter, which had a wonderful curriculum with an internship-based two-year syllabus. In effect, we basically changed our career paths due to the layoffs. She became a social worker and worked in various programs, including preschools, clinics and hospitals, until she became the district-wide social worker in the Levittown School District. I, meanwhile, was fortunate to quickly land a job as a school psychologist in the Bethpage School District, where I worked the next 35 years. I also became an adjunct professor at Queens College and started my own private practice in 1987. While I have retired from school life, I still maintain my private practice today as I write this. Going for my Ph.D. at the CUNY Graduate Center while working full time and raising two children was not easy and could not have been done without the support of Sue and the kids. I owe them incredible gratitude for enabling me to do this.

Trip to Israel (1979)

During the summer of 1979, my parents, along with my grandmother and Brenda, and Sue and I, flew to Israel, where we rented an apartment in Tel Aviv for several weeks. By this time, my mother was telling people that she considered Sue a daughter, not a daughter-in-law. We toured the entire country, and it was incredible. We met up with my grandfather, who flew in from Metz, France, and Victor and Suzy, who flew in from Liege, Belgium. They all came to help celebrate my mother's 50th birthday on August 10. We were in Haifa, where my maternal grandfather's brother, Binyamin Davidovic, and his wife lived. We also met up with friends of my parents, Aviva and Leon Bat, who helped us celebrate the occasion. As we were talking to Uncle Binyamin, a friend of his said he had a neighbor who had also been hidden by nuns in Belgium, just like my mother and Victor. He wrote down my mother's name and said he would inquire. The next day he asked my mother if her sister's name was Regine. My mother answered affirmatively, and the next evening, we were joined by the neighbor Uncle Binyamin's friend was referring to.

When she arrived, my mother immediately felt faint and had to sit down because she recognized the woman despite the 34 years that had passed since they last saw each other. The woman's name was Rita, and she and my mom immediately hugged each other and started crying. It turned out that Rita was the girl who had asked my mother shortly after she entered the convent/orphanage if she was Jewish, after which they became best friends. After my mother and her siblings were picked up by her parents when the war ended, my mother and Rita lost touch. She asked Rita how she'd ended up in Israel and also how her younger sister was doing. Rita told my mother that an uncle had found out about her and her sister several years after the war ended and had come to get them. However, because he was an uncle and not one of her parents, who did not survive the war, the nuns refused to give the uncle his two nieces. Instead, he arranged to kidnap them and take them to Israel—which he did. Rita had adjusted and eventually married and raised a family. Her sister, however, had not wanted to leave the convent as she was by that time a devout Catholic. She never was able to adjust to her uncle's Orthodox lifestyle and eventually died of what was termed a "broken heart." Again, I believe, a "broken heart" means giving up the will to live. My mother was incredibly shaken by all of this but at the same time so happy to see Rita after all those years. They would write to each other afterwards.

Another important event during our trip was meeting my parents' cousin Wolf (who was a first cousin to both my father and mother) and his family. Wolf Farkas was the son of my grandfather's oldest brother (Shlomo). Wolf had worked with my grandfather in the Carpathian Mountains and, after the war, had gone back to the area; however, the Russians would not allow him to leave once he was there. He'd married and had two sons, Shlomo and Avrum Meier, who grew up in the Soviet Union and served in the Soviet Army. When the Soviet Union eventually allowed Jews to emigrate in the 1970s, Wolf's family moved to Migdal Emek in Israel. There were hundreds of Russian emigres there by the time we visited them. Both Shlomo and Avrum Meier married, and Shlomo and his wife had a baby named Tzvikah, who was adorable. They had learned from others in Israel that there was a Farkas family in Queens, New York, who came from Czechoslovakia and it was they who reached out to my father.

Shortly thereafter, our trip to Israel was arranged. We spent a weekend with them—and we certainly weren't used to their Russian ways, especially having a whole fish and vodka for breakfast! They took us around the area and to Bethlehem as well. It was great to see my parents meeting up with family members from the old country who, like them, had survived the Holocaust.

Stories like this are not as uncommon as one might think, since most survivors were unable to return to their original homes after the war, and if they eventually were able to return, it was not until years later. In addition, if they *were* able to go back as Wolf Farkas did, they were sometimes unable to then *leave*. In any event, meeting Rita and then Uncle Wolf and his family was somewhat miraculous, considering 34 years had passed since the end of the war.

It was also my parents' and Sue's first trip to Israel and it proved to be incredible in every way. The scenery was so diverse, and the museums and religious sites, the ocean, desert and cities and, of course, Jerusalem were all places to behold. As was the Old City and the Western Wall.

I remember when Sue saw the Western Wall for the first time, you could see the emotion well up inside her. It was the same for my parents. I have always described Israel as the Bible come to life. Since I had already been there, I was sort of the travel guide. In addition, in the three weeks we were there, we had family and friends who took us to places we would not have known about.

I did become sick the last few days of the trip because I stupidly drank what seemed like fresh water from a swimming hole in the Negev. The next day, we rented a car and Sue, my father and I took off early to visit Rachel's Tomb, the Ein Gedi nature reserve (where you hike to a waterfall), the Dead Sea and Hebron, the site of the Kever Avot (the tomb of the forefathers, where Abraham, Isaac and Jacob are believed to have been buried). I felt fine in the morning but within a few hours, was feeling nauseous. The smell of the mud baths by the Dead Sea, which Sue and my father thoroughly enjoyed, only made me more sick. When we got to Hebron, it was prayer time for those who were Muslims, so we couldn't enter the site. I collapsed on a bench, feeling really weak. Afterwards, I drove us to Rachel's Tomb, at which time my digestive system exploded. However, I also realized the bathroom I had fled to had no toilet paper. Sue had to ask the soldiers guarding the tomb for some, and when I finally emerged from the bathroom, they were laughing.

That night, I ran a fever and almost passed out. I was taken to the emergency room at the nearest hospital and the doctors confirmed the obvious—a bad case of *"shil shul,"* Hebrew for diarrhea.

I was sick in bed in the apartment the last few days of the vacation.

When we came home to New York City after an incredibly long flight, I was still weak. That night, I woke up after a terrible dream that I was in the desert in Israel and sweating from the heat. I was glad to realize that I was actually in my own bed. However, when Sue took my temperature, I was running a high fever, and we took a taxi a few blocks to the Lenox Hill Hospital emergency room. They said I was dehydrated and wanted to admit me, but I refused so they hooked me up to an IV. When the bag was finished, they felt I was healthy enough to go home. Still, I was weak for several more days after that. The takeaway from this: don't drink the water anywhere if it is not out of a closed and/or capped bottle.

9

ELISSA AND ERIC AND GRANDCHILDREN

SUE AND I WERE BY THEN LIVING in a Manhattan apartment on East 77th Street. We enjoyed being in the city, and the apartment was huge, but it did not have much sunlight. We had first seen it during the 45 minutes the sun actually streamed in through the foyer window, and we loved it because of its size—it contained a bedroom, an eat-in kitchen and a huge foyer in which we were able to put a dining room table and a desk, as well as a sewing machine. We were on the second floor of a pre-war building, in the back. Sue worked in Kingsbrook Medical Center in Brooklyn, and I commuted to my job in Bethpage along with Maura Olson and Gerry Dalven, who also worked at Central Boulevard School. The commutes were incredibly interesting as we shared details about our lives during the one-hour rides back and forth.

Gerry was a fountain of knowledge who could expound on everything from architecture to plants to trees and on practically everything else we passed on our trips to and from work. He also seemed to know everybody. We'd pass a billboard displaying the Marlboro Man cowboy, and he would say, "That's my friend Joe," from somewhere. We sometimes thought he was making it all up but, eventually, we *met* all these people. The joke was, there were these tourists in Rome who went to Vatican City and looked up where the masses were gazing, and they said: "Who is up there blessing the people with Gerry Dalven?"

Around this time, Sue and I decided we wanted to start a family. Luckily, all went well, and we learned Sue was pregnant shortly after we started trying. We didn't know the sex of the baby because we wanted to be surprised. We also couldn't wait to tell our parents once some time had passed. We picked up Sue's parents to bring them to my parents to tell them together, and on the way, Sue's father asked us when we were going to provide them with a grandchild. Needless to say, our parents were thrilled to learn they would become grandparents. I was lucky to have met Dr. Peter Cohen through my brother. Peter was a psychologist doing research on fathers to be. He was a member of the Cafh group, along with Eddie. We met several times in the months before Elissa was born, and it was incredibly therapeutic to discuss how my parents raised us and how differently I hoped to raise my own children. I can recall discussing that I wanted to be very involved in all aspects of my children's lives from changing their diapers and feeding them to throwing a ball with them or encouraging their talents and interests. While my parents were not that involved in our daily activities when my brother, sister and I were growing up, I always felt loved and cared for. But I wanted to be more engaged than they had been.

On March 11, 1981, we went to the hospital because Sue was

having contractions and we were told to go home and wait for a while. We came back later in the day, and after 19 hours of labor, Elissa Wertheim Farkas was born at 12:36 a.m. on March 12.

We immediately fell in love with her. She was absolutely beautiful, and we were elated. Seeing her being born was truly a miracle. That morning, I made dozens of calls to share the good news with our friends and family while Sue was with Elissa in the room. I stayed in the hospital all day, and at night I went to our apartment to put together the crib and baby furniture that had been delivered. My brother, Eddie, had built a wall to provide a space for Elissa to have a crib, dresser and changing table in our bedroom. It was a small room, but it burst with warmth and love for our new baby. It was decorated with clown decor made by some teachers in my school and Sue's mother.

Our parents and Brenda were in love with Elissa as well. We had waited six years after we were married to have our first child, and this was puzzling to our parents who had babies (Sue and me) within about a year after they were married. But now that they were grandparents, they were overjoyed. Sue's father's family had left Germany in the late 1930s and Sue's mother had escaped Germany to join her sister, Aunt Edith, in the United States in 1940. As you have already read, my parents survived the Holocaust and lost many family members, as did the family of Sue's mother. For them, repopulating the Jewish race after the terrible losses inflicted by the Holocaust was an imperative. And living long enough to have grandchildren and, in the case of my maternal grandmother, Babi, who lived with my parents, and my paternal grandfather (Old Zeide), who visited and lived with my parents for over a year, being alive to see the birth of their great-grandchildren was an enormous "*zchius*" or honor.

It was wonderful to see how much our parents loved being with Elissa and later with Eric as well. They had been so busy trying to build a life for themselves and us that they had no time to play when we were kids. My father worked several jobs and my mother took care of us. So watching them get down on the floor and rolling a ball with Elissa and Eric was wonderful.

Brenda is 11 years younger than I am, and I cannot recall seeing my parents on the floor playing with her either. That was something Eddie and I did with her.

So I feel my parents were much more in the moment and able to really be with their grandchildren than when they were raising their own children. In some ways, the arrival of grandchildren provided affirmation, to Holocaust survivors who had lost so much family, that life goes on. It was also evocative of the *shtetl*, where having three or four or even five generations of family living in close proximity was not unusual.

Sue took a maternity leave to stay home with Elissa as I continued to commute to Bethpage. Our friends, family and colleagues created a warm and loving environment for Elissa and it seemed for several months that we were getting new baby gifts daily. I would get off the train at Lexington and 77th Street, and Sue and Elissa would frequently meet me for the walk home to our apartment. We loved the city and frequented Central Park, Gracie Square Park and the Ducky Park down the street from our apartment. We also traveled with Elissa in the summertime to bed-and-breakfasts in the Northeast and also to California to visit our friends. But the best was watching our parents' joy when we came to visit or sleep over with Elissa and later Eric.

As Elissa grew, we brought in more and more baby furniture, such as a playpen, a swing and all the books and toys one gets for a toddler. Her stuff was soon taking over the apartment, and we knew we would have to move to a house. The summer of 1982 was a particularly hot and humid one in New York City. Going out with her was stifling and a lot of the city was not particularly clean and well-maintained.

That summer, we visited and stayed with our friend Leigh in Northern California, where Elissa had her own room and we parked the car in front of the house instead of looking for parking in the city. It convinced us to buy a house.

Sue and I started considering a move to Long Island, since I was working there. She would make appointments with a realtor. and we looked at houses in Northport, Huntington, Melville and then Plainview. We saw many houses, some of them bigger than the one we finally bought in Plainview. However, we didn't especially like some of the areas where we drove around. We couldn't see ourselves living there. When we looked in Plainview, we felt it was more in line with our values and needs, not the least of which was having a sizable Jewish community. Plainview had several synagogues, kosher butchers, kosher restaurants and so on. One day I went during my lunch hour to see the house we finally bid on and bought, and I called Sue to have her come out with Elissa to look at it. As soon as Sue saw it, she loved it, and I recall telling her to calm down as we were going to be negotiating with the owners to buy it. We loved the house and could see how it would serve our needs and it was only a 10-to-12-minute commute to my school in Bethpage. The street was tree-lined and lush, as it was the middle of spring. We also saw a lot of young children on the block, including Thomas, who lived across the street. He introduced himself to us when we were looking at the house and invited us to live with him until we moved into our house. The fact that there were so many children made this a great block, since Elissa would obviously have other children to play with.

Move to Plainview

After we bought the house, Sue and I painted and wallpapered it with the help of Brenda and Maura Olson, a teacher I worked with. I would come over during my lunch hour and water the front yard and the back and do some painting. On the weekends, we would all show up to paint, do some fixing up and buy stuff for the house, such as hoses, garbage pails, a lawn mower, and so on. These were things we had not planned for but had to purchase. We hired a carpenter from my school district who designed and built bookcases in the guest room, which we, including Elissa, painted.

On July 1, 1983, we moved in. It was beautiful and sunny that weekend, and we loved being outside, surrounded by the trees in our backyard. We had bought a charcoal grill and a round wooden picnic table that we had kept under the bed in our apartment. We also bought a swing set for Elissa, which we hired somebody to put together and anchor into the ground. It had two swings, a teeter-totter and a seat for two facing each other to swing back and forth. The kids used it for years.

We immediately felt at home in the house despite the fact we didn't have furniture for the living room and only our kitchen table for the dining room. Our large couch couldn't fit into the room we initially used as the den (this later became Eric's room) to watch TV. So the couch sat alone in the living room until we moved it into the unfinished basement for the kids to have another place to play. The only rooms that were furnished were our bedroom, Elissa's bedroom and the guest room with the bookcases. We bought Elissa a trundle bed, so a friend would be able to sleep over, and we purchased a new dresser for her as well. We also had the carpenter make a built-in desk area for her.

One time before we moved in, I went over to water the lawn. I used the nozzle and watered the back and then the front. I was soaked, so I put down the hose since no water came out because I wasn't pressing the nozzle. I changed my clothes and went back to our apartment in the city.

The next day, I came to do some more work and water the front lawn, as it was really hot. Our next-door neighbor came out to introduce himself and told me he'd shut off our water the day before in order to avert a flood because the hose had burst—the problem being that I had never shut off the water when I left.

I thanked him and figured he must have thought I was a knucklehead. I was learning about being a homeowner on the fly. In the years that followed, I watered and mowed the lawn myself since we couldn't afford to pay a landscaper. I enjoyed doing these tasks because I could see the finished product. It was different than my job, where cases were almost always ongoing. Similarly, I preferred reading magazines and articles during the school year to reading books, which required a greater investment of time.

We had Gary and Babs along with their families over as our first guests in our new house. We had a wonderful time entertaining them and showing them our house. However, after the July 4th weekend, we realized there were no children on the block during the day: All of them had been signed up for day camp. We hadn't realized that everyone went to day camp, so we'd never thought about signing Elissa up. As a result, she had nobody to play with until later in the afternoon when the block was teeming with kids.

This never occurred again—we always signed the kids up for

day camp. The local Camp Apollo program was run in conjunction with the Plainview school district. It was the best deal in town.

We also needed to get some kind of day care for Elissa for September since Sue had to go back to work. We had loved her day-care situation in Manhattan with Liz and Isabel. They were a warm, loving mother-and-daughter team who took in several other children Elissa really got along with. Elissa was by far the most talkative one there, and she would tell us everything that happened. Several teachers I worked with told me about Mrs. Fournier, who had a day care program in her basement in Bethpage. It was fine for a while, but when she decided to toilet-train Elissa without our permission, we decided to pull her out and enroll her in Rainbow Hill Nursery School, which she loved. They admitted her despite the fact she was under 3 years old because she was so verbal and capable.

When I started working in Bethpage in 1977, I initially worked in the Charles Campagne School, where the special education classes were situated. When the administration proposed moving the classes to the Central Boulevard School, the special-education parents were in an uproar. They felt their children were with people who knew them and had been able to establish programs that worked. The administration decided I would join the students in the move to the Central Boulevard School (CBS) and that made the parents happy. I basically was a throw-in in the trade. I was reluctant to move, because I had gained the trust of the principal at Charles Campagne, a woman named Mary Quinn. Furthermore, the principal at CBS, Kenny Blau, liked his school psychologist and showed no reluctance in telling me so.

But it turned out to be a fantastic move for all, as I got to work with Kenny, who turned out to be very supportive and allowed me to set up my job as I saw fit. We became very close, and he was largely responsible for giving me the freedom to make the position multifaceted and of utmost importance in the school. I was a proactive psychologist, not a reactive psychologist. CBS had early hours, so I was able to get home by 3:00 in the afternoon to meet Elissa and Eric when they got off the bus and, as they got older, pick them up from middle school. Subsequently, every other principal and director of special education I worked with relied on me and let me do my job as I deemed fit. Getting home early also allowed me to start my private practice as early as 3:15 in the afternoon.

I also worked for the New York City Board of Education every summer after I graduated in 1977. I would work for six weeks each summer in a district where I was assigned to do psychological evaluations and reports. I worked in some horrible neighborhoods where you really couldn't walk alone. We would be told to wait in the train station until there were several of us to walk together the few blocks to the school that we were working in. And if I drove, I had to essentially pay to park on the street, even though there were no meters. On the first day I used my car, some guy asked me to pay him $10 to watch it. Initially, I said, "No thanks." When I got to my car later that afternoon, I had two slashed tires. The guy was there and told me where I could get two new tires. I reluctantly concluded that $10.00 a day was a good investment because replacing those two tires cost me almost $200.00. Some of the students I evaluated during those summers had such hard lives it made me appreciate how easy working in Bethpage was in comparison.

I did these summer testing sessions for 10 years, from 1977 to 1987. I was lucky to then spend the next 25 summers in the Plainview-Old Bethpage Summer Special Education Program. I conducted student groups, parent groups and parent-education programs and also worked with students, teachers and aides on a daily basis. More important, I made lifelong friends, including Ellie Becker, John Iorio, Pat Eschausse, George Manolakes and Sue Corallo. One of the best experiences was the four summers I worked alongside Eric in the program. He got to see me working as a psychologist and I was able to see him interact with the students as well.

In the summers, I would get home around 2:30 in the afternoon to be with Sue and the kids. At the end of August, we always took a family vacation. We were lucky to travel to Europe, Israel, Hawaii and Mexico, and to California many times, and to take a great cross-country trip in which we stayed at Steve Ross's house in Boulder, Colorado, as our home base. Summers were great for the whole family.

Back to 1983: Sue and I were ready for our second child and, thankfully, we were blessed with the arrival of Eric Bradley Farkas on August 28, 1984. He weighed 8 pounds 8 ounces. He was a wonderful second child except for the fact he had his days and nights confused for the first several months after he was born. I can recall coming home and asking Sue how long he had been up during the day, since that would indicate how our nights would go. He eventually got that all squared away, and then we had our girl and our boy. Some call this a king's family and we felt blessed and enriched by our two children. Sue and I were very attentive to, and enjoyed all that we did with, them. Elissa was a great big sister, and Eric was entertained just watching Elissa be Elissa, as she was always creating scenes and singing or dancing in front of him. And while Elissa was a terrific big sister, Eric was an incredible younger brother as he allowed her to have the spotlight.

Our parents now had two grandchildren too, and they were enthralled by them. We would have them over to our house for barbecues and we would visit them in their homes as well. We often slept over, especially for Passover seders and other holidays. My father would see us come in with all our stuff, and he would joke that we seemed to be planning to come for a week or a month instead of two days. The kids would sleep in my parents' room and hop onto their bed in the morning. My grandmother was there as well. Brenda was still living at home, and she was a terrific aunt to them. Sue and I and the kids would go to *shul* with my parents and my grandfather, who was living with my parents for a few years. He was wise enough to calm my father when Elissa sat on the *bima* with the rabbi. His thinking was to make coming to *shul* fun, so the kids would want to keep coming back. If little ones had to just sit and be quiet, they would get bored.

Interestingly enough, my father was trying to respect what he thought my grandfather would want because my grandfather was very Orthodox. In fact, my grandfather realized that enjoying an experience makes you want to do it again, especially when you are young.

Almost all parents and grandparents are filled with joy in welcoming newborns into the family, but Holocaust survivors are particularly thrilled. My parents and grandparents were ecstatic when their grandchildren were born. I think it meant more to them in the sense that the family was replenishing the tremendous losses from the Holocaust, and it was a chance to name the grandchildren after lost parents and siblings. I was named Hershel (Tzvi) after a great-grandfather, Hersh Sobel. Eddie was named Yehuda Baruch after our maternal great-grandfather, Jutko Davidovic. Brenda was named Brana Pava after our paternal grandmother, Brana Farkas *née* Sobel and paternal/maternal great-grandmother, Pava Farkas.

Elissa is named Yael Rivka after Sue's mother's sister and my father's oldest sister, who both died in the Holocaust. Eric is named Efraim Bentzion after my maternal grandfather, Efraim, and my father's brother, Bentzion, who died in the Holocaust. Sammy, my sister Brenda's son, is named after our paternal grandfather, Samuel. In Ashkenazi tradition, the Hebrew name honors the deceased and their memory, and in that way, their soul lives on through that child. The hope is the positive attributes of the deceased will be instilled in the child. Some believe this tradition dates back to a biblical verse: "Like his name, so is he."

I am glad to say our children grew up visiting both sets of grandparents frequently and that they enjoyed the love their grandparents heaped upon them. They would sleep over at both houses, and every February school vacation we would spend a week in Florida with my parents. As it was, my parents were frequent travelers to see family in Europe and also traveled with their friends, Joe, Gilda, Aviva and Leon, across the United States and Canada. And they also went to Florida every winter, often with family and friends. When Brenda bought an apartment in North Miami Beach, they went there for many years after Thanksgiving and stayed until after Passover—until my father's Alzheimer's and my mother's cancer made traveling too difficult. As I mentioned, my parents were much more involved in playing with their grandchildren than they were with me, Eddie and Brenda when we were growing up. Perhaps it had to do with where they were in their lives. I never questioned this at the time because nobody I knew had parents who threw a ball around—they were all immigrants and, for the most part, Holocaust survivors. As I got older and met more Americanized parents, I realized what I had missed and wished it had been different.

Of course, when my parents became grandparents, they were more settled and not working several jobs, and my father was no longer a slave to his store. They were more able to enjoy the fruits of their labor and find time to play with their grandchildren and to laugh with them and get *"nachas"* from watching them be who they were. It was a pleasure to see this, to watch my father sit with them and get a kick out of their silly behavior—except when they made too much noise at the *seders*. Years later, I would watch him sit in his car with Sammy, in the garage at Brenda's house, and just let Sammy pretend he was driving the car. Elissa would often say my mother was her pal as they would watch sitcoms like *Full House* and *Who's the Boss?* My parents put aside sugary cereals like Trix for them, which we never had growing up. Eric could make my father laugh by imitating him and/or rubbing his belly. My father's playful pet name for Eric was *"Chayela"* or *"Vilda Chaya"* (wild animal). Elissa and Eric looked forward to sleepovers with my parents, with or without Sue and me. Seeing my parents playing and laughing like that made me realize how much they had changed and were able to enjoy things much more than they had in the past. They were also able to laugh with their friends and at family gatherings. However, at home growing up during a typical day with them, it was not as joyful and loose for us. It was more practical.

Elissa and Eric experienced them very differently—it was a mutual love affair between grandparents and grandchildren. My mother would take them to McDonald's to play in the playground there, and my father would take them to the local Purim festival so they could go on rides. And they all had a great time, too, when they were in Florida and my parents took Elissa and Eric to Denny's and the movies. There is no question, my parents enjoyed their later years and lived life more fully and in the moment. I am certain it is because they were able to joyfully experience being grandparents, and it thrilled Sue and me to see this.

Elissa, meanwhile, was becoming smart, funny and creative and someone who was willing to try anything. This belied her somewhat shy tendencies. It took her a little while to warm up to a situation, but once warm, she took charge. She loved to watch TV shows and old movies, especially musicals. It was no surprise she loved Broadway musicals. She didn't just learn the songs of these musicals—she learned the lines, too. She was musically inclined, had artistic talent from a young age and loved acting. When she was in kindergarten, we signed her up to try out for a part in a play by the Paper Bag Players at our local library. It turned out that she was the only child who was trying out; everyone else was an adult. She got the part and ended up being the star of the show. Elissa also made up her own skits and assigned parts to Eric and the children of some of our family friends. She would feed them lines, which often came from plays in which she knew all the lines. At the dinner table, she often assigned Sue, Eric and me to write compositions, and then, as "Mrs. B," the teacher, would give us grades for our efforts. She played about 10 other parts in Mrs. B's class. When her best friend, Mara, came over, she had a part for her as well. We would laugh through the meals. Elissa also had lots of friends and did extremely well in school. She was always a wonderful big sister to Eric. They would fight and argue at times, but in general, she made it easy for him, especially as he followed her into elementary, middle and high school and then to the University of Michigan. Her friends would always say "hi" to Eric, and he enjoyed the "cool" of having an older sister and being friends with her friends. Eric was outgoing and friendly from a very young age. As a toddler, he might go over to another adult on line in the bagel store and say,

"The Mets winned last night." The adult would smile and respond. He wasn't a good student at first through no fault of his own, as he was unfortunately being taught with the experimental Whole Language approach, which did not include phonics or sight words. Thus, he didn't read until the middle of second grade, when his teacher used the standard reading curriculum that *did* use both. He needed to work a little harder than Elissa, who seemed to learn by just listening in class.

However, he became an excellent student as well. Eric was a good athlete and very competitive. He played numerous sports and was an excellent soccer player through high school. In essence, Eric was funny and carefree while growing up, especially with his grandparents and could entertain them with his silliness. Our parents adored Elissa and Eric and couldn't get enough of them. They in turn, were extremely loving with their grandparents.

A Bat Mitzvah and then a Bar Mitzvah

The bat and bar mitzvah celebrations for Elissa and Eric stand out for different reasons. Elissa chose Broadway plays as her theme for her bat mitzvah. She basically did everything—with a little bit of help from Sue. At some point, we spoke to a friend of ours, Michael Bruh, who had access to printing and designing programs and, along with Elissa, wrote and created a Playbill for all the guests. In it, she introduced the tables by the musical representing the table and told a little bit about everyone at the table. The playbill was incredible and combined much of Elissa's artistic and creative abilities as well as her friendly and loving spirit.

Eric chose sports teams as his bar mitzvah theme. He helped organize it, and we rented the same venue as the one we used for

Elissa's bat mitzvah.

Unfortunately, Sue's dad (Pa) passed away a week before the bar mitzvah. During the *shiva* we spoke to Eric about how we would have to change everything for his bar mitzvah because Sue wouldn't be able to hear music during her year of mourning. We would have to change the venue to a luncheon at Plainview Jewish Center. This also meant no pictures, videos or candle-lighting. When he heard this, he immediately burst out crying. We comforted him, and he said he understood why this had to happen and he would be O.K. While we did not have music and pictures because it was the Sabbath, Eric was able to have a candle-lighting ceremony of sorts by inserting flags in the cake. Eric came through as the *mensch* he always was and is and, as I noted at his wedding, we were glad to see him finally have the big celebration with music, cameras and video that he wasn't able to have at his bar mitzvah. Sue and I are grateful we have two children who are truly good and loving people. These two rites of passage when they turned 13 years of age were incredibly meaningful as we shared them with our family and friends—including Uncle Moishe, Aunt Rosette and Dany, who came from Metz—and the love in the room was palpable.

A few years before his bar mitzvah, Eric started collecting autographs when we went to Yankee, Met or Knick games. He had a knack of getting the players to sign something. He also was able to get baseballs from the players, which were eventually signed by them. Once he got Vai Sikahema of the Philadelphia Eagles to give him the football he had been practicing with prior to the game. Eric kept calling, "Mr. Sikahema, Mr. Sikahema!" and he came over and spoke to Eric, saying, "Even though you're a Giants fan, here's the ball."

Another time, Cal Ripken was stretching in the grass behind third base. At the time he had just broken Lou Gehrig's legendary record for consecutive games played. Eric ran over to the box seats near where Ripken was stretching and somehow got to the front of a throng of autograph-seekers. When he was done stretching, Ripken went over and signed one item—Eric's! He was now the proud owner of a picture that depicted Ripken and Lou Gehrig as "Ironmen" and was autographed by Ripken.

I often helped him when he was attempting to add to his autographs, and he had an incredible collection. When he went off to college, Eric and I couldn't go to many Knicks games anymore, since his schedule didn't allow it. I found I missed this part of our bonding and began getting autographs by mail, as well as before and after games. At this point, there are several thousand autographs in our collection. I loved going to games with Eric, as well as with Elissa and Sue, because I never went to any sporting event with my parents. Sports was something I pretty much did with my friends, and there was no parental involvement.

10

SIMCHAS AND SICKNESS

Weddings

AFTER SUE AND I MARRIED on December 22, 1974, Brenda, my sister, was next to marry. She wed Dan Bacharach on January 3, 1987. She had been dating him for quite a while before they got engaged. Their marriage was a *"simcha"* (joyous celebration) shared with family and friends. Brenda was the baby of the family and the daughter my parents wanted after two sons.

Initially, I was the baby-sitter for her and Eddie when we lived in Bensonhurst. She was 6 years old when my parents bought their house in Queens, and it is the home where Brenda grew up. I was in college and Eddie was in high school at the time, and we both moved out by the time Brenda was 10 or 11 years old. In effect, she grew up in part as an only child since Eddie, Sue and I would visit but did not live there. Sue and I were like surrogate parents to her and visited her at camp when it was visiting day and my parents were in Europe. We also would take Brenda on camping trips when she was a teenager, and she turned out to be an incredible aunt when Elissa and Eric were born.

My parents were so happy for Brenda that she was getting married, and welcomed Dan into the family. They were warm and friendly to his parents as well. We often spent Mother's Day and Father's Day with our parents, as well as Sue's parents and Dan's. We also went camping with Brenda and Dan, and Elissa and Eric loved spending time with them. The kids would stay over at their house in Long Branch and go to the beach and a nearby amusement park.

And my parents loved making the wedding because it meant their family and friends would all be together to celebrate, dance, catch up with one another and share a good time. Sue was Brenda's matron of honor, and Elissa was the flower girl who also sang "May We Wish You the Happiest Marriage" from *Babes in Toyland*. Elissa loved musicals and learned all the songs. It seems like Zachy, who is Elissa and Ben's son, already has the same love and talent at age 3. Unfortunately, Brenda and Dan's marriage ended in divorce after 10 years, which resulted in our family feeling another loss. My parents felt bad for Brenda, as did Sue and I, and Elissa and Eric lost a fun uncle.

My brother, Eddie, had gone to live on a commune in Cali, Colombia a few months before Sue and I married. He was with several other men at the commune, and it was in many ways a search for meaning for him and the others through Cafh, an organization dedicated to spiritual enlightenment that Eddie loved and was very involved in for the rest of his life. Sue and I went to several meetings of Cafh and met several of his friends, who were very friendly and very smart.

My parents, especially my mother, were hurt by Eddie's departure to Colombia. I think she experienced feelings of abandonment and loss when he left, feelings she would again experience when Brenda decided to go away to college. She didn't understand why Eddie would go to Cali instead of going to Israel to live on a kibbutz. Eddie didn't do a good job of explaining his decision either. I suspect they never would have understood his spiritual questioning and quest.

Nevertheless, when Eddie invited them to come to Cali, they took Brenda with them and visited him. Eddie was very smart, well read and had a great deal of knowledge but he had difficulty picking up social cues. He was respected in Cafh and had many friends there. Years later, when we visited him in his home in Ecuador, we could see that he was highly regarded by the people there as well.

Growing up, Eddie did not have many friends. I don't recall him going to their homes when we lived in Brooklyn, or inviting them over. When we moved to Queens and he attended Jamaica High School, he had one friend, Nathan, with whom he hung out. He may have had others in high school, but they never came to our house, which Nathan did.

Eddie left for Colombia after his sophomore year in college, and when he returned in December 1980, six years later, he went back to school for his engineering degree and became quite proficient in his field. He was a project manager for several companies, and also did work for the Port Authority at LaGuardia Airport. In 1988, he met Marianna Alvandian on jury duty. She worked for Finnair, the airline of Finland, and as far as I know, she was his first relationship. My parents were not enamored with her since she was not Jewish, and Eddie was aware of that. He married her on February 16, 1989, in a civil ceremony in the courthouse in Queens, and he asked me to be his witness. My parents were in Florida at the time. He told them he was married when he met them at the airport when they returned from their Florida vacation several months later. They were shocked he had married without telling them or inviting them. Although my parents were not in favor of the marriage, they chose to keep their relationship with Eddie on solid footing, welcomed Marianna and her parents to their home and became quite amiable with her parents. This was very different from the way my Uncle Benny reacted when his son, Morris, married Jer, who is lovely, respectful and smart and more importantly, perfect for Morris. But she was not Jewish, and Benny refused to visit them in their beautiful home; my aunt Regine, along with my mother, had to meet them secretly. Marianna, meanwhile, initially came to Passover seders and other gatherings at my parents' house, but later, Eddie would come alone, saying she didn't feel well. We later found out, after Eddie divorced her in December of 2005, that Marianna was often depressed. This was not atypical of Eddie's communication with our family. He felt bad that he divorced her and sent her alimony way past when he had to. Eddie had a big heart, but his communication with the family at times was lacking.

A number of years later he met Jenny Noboa, who was a student in a project-management class he was teaching. He married her on November 15, 2009, in a ceremony attended by our family and Jenny's in a restaurant. She made him very happy and he looked better than he had in years. They eventually moved to Ecuador, where she was from, and they bought a beautiful apartment in Salinas overlooking the ocean. When Sue and I visited them, he and

Jenny were gracious hosts and loved showing us around Ecuador and introducing us to other family members and their friends. It was great to see him this way. Eddie probably should have been born in South America, as he seemed most comfortable there.

Meanwhile, after several years and several relationships, Brenda met Bill Vega and they dated for a while. Brenda had done well professionally, working in marketing, and owned a house in Westhampton and the apartment in North Miami Beach, where my parents stayed for many years to get through the bitter New York winters. She and Bill lived in Stuyvesant Town in Manhattan, and Sammy was born several months into their relationship. At my parents' urging, Brenda and Bill married. My parents spent a great deal of time with them in Westhampton and loved playing with Sammy. They loved Brenda becoming a mother and giving them another grandchild. Unfortunately, Bill had serious issues, which led to their divorce and his continued absence in Sammy's life.

Cancer and Alzheimer's

In 1991, my mother retired from working as the dietician in the New Glen Oaks Nursing Home, which was owned by my uncle Avrum. A few months later, Leah, a friend down the block, asked her to go with her for a mammogram. Leah was divorced and was often at my parents' house to just chat. She became a regular at my parents' seders and other holiday gatherings. My mother asked my aunt Regine to come along as well.

My mother had never had a mammogram and, at 62, was really going along just to keep Leah company. In the end, all three of them had their mammograms done.

Several days later, Leah and Regine were told everything was fine. My mother, however, learned she had breast cancer and would need to have surgery.

She was devastated and kept saying, "Why me?" Sue and I got the names of a well-known radiation oncologist as well as the oncologist who would go on to treat her until her death at age 88.

Years later, when I started taking care of my parents' finances and other paperwork they could no longer manage, I found a psychiatric report, from the time when my mother was diagnosed with cancer, that stated she was depressed and needed to be put on medication. Whether she took the meds or not, I do not know. I was shocked because, beyond her initial expression of "Why me?" we did not see her struggling to accept the situation.

Furthermore, I was a psychologist and Sue was a social worker, and she never spoke to either of us about any emotional issues she was having.

Perhaps she did not want us to worry, but I was stunned to find that report. My mother did end up having surgery, along with seven weeks of daily radiation and chemotherapy, and she dealt with it quite bravely. She seemed to be a real trouper and still wanted Elissa and Eric to sleep over at their house and visit her and my father in Florida, and she wanted to live the life she had always lived.

My father was also shaken by her diagnosis. He was afraid of losing her and he prayed for her. He made a deal with God to heal her and get her through the surgery and radiation. If God healed her, and got her through surgery, he would go to *shul* every day for both the morning and evening *minyans*. He did this for the next 20-plus years until Alzheimer's got the best of him. Since he went to *shul* twice a day, he was often asked by family and friends and sometimes our friends to say Kaddish for someone's deceased relative for the next 11 months. He did this mitzvah gladly.

My mother's cancer eventually went into remission but returned in her later years as it metastasized to her spine and bones. She was still always open to doing things with us and going places at a moment's notice. She fought cancer the way she dealt with everything else, not giving in and doing what she wanted to do. When it was really bad at the end and I asked Dr. Marino, her oncologist, how much time she really had left, he told me, "I don't know. I thought she would be dead a year ago. She is a fighter."

She made goals at the end. She wanted to dance at Eric's wedding, then at Elissa's wedding, then she wanted to see Sienna (Eric and Jess' daughter and her great-granddaughter) be born, then she wanted to see Zachy (Elissa and Ben's son and her great-grandson) be born. She said that she wanted to live to be at Sammy's *bar mitzvah* but she wasn't sure if she would make it (and, unfortunately, she didn't).

Those goals helped her to keep fighting the pain from the cancer, the arthritis, the spinal stenosis and her atrial fibrillation, which often resulted in trips to the emergency room.

Her determination and spirit were inspiring. In May 2020, I was diagnosed with mantle cell lymphoma. I was shocked at the diagnosis, because I was feeling fine at the time. I firmly believe I have channeled my parents' determination and strength to help me face my medical situation and continue to do what I have to do to beat it. At this time, the fight goes on.

While my mother was dealing with her cancer, and the pain made it harder for her to walk and do the things she always did, my father started to decline cognitively and was diagnosed with Alzheimer's. At first, it was repeating himself and not remembering things that had just occurred. Several times he got lost and could not remember how to get home from *shul* after the morning *minyan*. Thankfully, others knew him and got him home. Eventually, somebody volunteered to pick him up and drop him off for morning *minyans*. He stopped going in the afternoon because there was nobody to pick him up and the walk became too much for my mother.

She also worried a great deal about him walking out of the house, and that she wouldn't be able to chase him. As a result, he was basically confined to be with her in the den so she could keep track of him. If he got up, she demanded to know where he was going, and he would get angry. I had already retired from my job as a school psychologist, but I continued to teach in the school psychology program at Queens College and still maintained my private practice. Over the years, I had helped train well over 100 school psychologists as an adjunct lecturer, field supervisor and university supervisor at Queens. I loved it and felt I was giving something back. The salary was not great but the sense that I was training young people to do these important jobs was very satisfying.

But my parents' health was deteriorating more and more, and I realized I had to give up my teaching position at Queens in order to give more time to my parents.

Eventually, they needed aides around the clock since neither could really help the other. We were lucky to get some really devoted aides, such as Ndeye, who was from Senegal. She spoke French and thought of my mother like a mother. She could enlist her cooperation. My mother was fiercely independent and hated when anybody told her what to do. She ended up giving Ndeye various gifts, including some of her own jewelry. There were other aides, like Julie, who stayed overnight for several years and would not leave until the morning aide came. If the aide did not show up, she would stay with my parents. Brenda and I were all too often on the phone with the agency to rectify the situation when aides did not show up, or to get other aides assigned when the regular aide was off or on vacation. Julie, meanwhile, was devoted to my parents, and because she did not let my mother bully her to get out of eating, drinking or walking, there was sometimes friction between them. And I would go over once or twice a week and do all their shopping, set up their medications and, in general, organize everything for the next few days.

At times, I would take them to their doctor appointments separately, so my mother could get a break from worrying about my father. When I took her out to lunch, she would invariably tell me to call the house to make sure my father was OK. You would never have known she cared and worried about him so much because there were times she would yell at him for just sitting and not watching the television show (usually the news) that she was watching. She would get angry at his overall decline, and she didn't comprehend the severity of his dementia. He would often respond by saying, "Why are you yelling?"

Throughout these tough years, one could see how much they loved each other. When my mother was hospitalized on one occasion, my father would go to a window of the house and look out, awaiting her arrival, and constantly ask where she was.

One day, I brought him to the hospital, and when he walked in and saw her, he said, "Oh, here you are. I was missing you." He then bent down and kissed her. Sue, Brenda and I started crying.

There were other times when he was able to surprise us by pulling it together and behaving as he always had. But there weren't enough of those times, and it was hard to watch him decline to the point of being like a toddler. Growing up and seeing him knock out handmade suits and dresses with artistry and then, all those years later, play with an Alzheimer's Fidget Blanket that had buttons to close and zippers to zip on it, was heartbreaking. Still, throughout his illness he always knew who Esther was. Eventually, he did not recognize his children, or his brother when Uncle Moishe visited him, but he asked about Esther all the time.

The last few years, I went over weekly to shower him, as he hated the shower and would get physical when anyone tried to get him to take one. Julie and I would get him in the shower, and it would be a struggle, with him kicking and punching me the entire time. But once I turned off the water, helped him out of the shower and gave him a towel, he would say, "Thank you, thank you." He was openly friendly, as if the previous 10–15 minutes had never happened. All the aides told us how easy he was to care for and what a nice man he was. Thank goodness they never had to shower him or cut his nails. But in the end, those were minor things. For even in the throes of Alzheimer's, he was still a mensch who had a warm countenance about him.

Grandchildren Get Married, and Great-Grandchildren Are Born

When Eric introduced my parents to Jess, and then Elissa did the same with Ben, they immediately welcomed them and their families as members of our family. My mother always referred to Jess as "Jessie" in an affectionate way. Nobody else except Val, Jess's mother, called her that, and my mother hadn't even met Val at that point. My parents loved celebrations such as their grandchildren's bat or bar mitzvahs and especially their weddings. Both of them were in better health for Eric and Jess's wedding, so it was easy for them to participate and it was quite enjoyable. (I should also add that Eric gave me a great and unforgettable honor by asking me to be his best man at his wedding.)

However, the same situation did not exist by the time Elissa and Ben got married. My dad's Alzheimer's and my mom's cancer had advanced to the point that they were a concern and worry to Sue and me. We hoped and prayed they would make it to the wedding and would have no issues. My mother could barely walk by then, but she had promised Elissa she would dance at her wedding and she did. There is a video of my mother and me doing the *hora* while she is holding on to her walker—and I'm holding onto it as well to make sure she doesn't fall. And yet, she tossed the walker away so she could dance without it. And she did, dancing with Elissa, Eric and others as if she were healthy. If that wasn't enough, all of a sudden, my father was on the dance floor as well, and he started to dance, too. At the end of the evening, when my father was leaving, he went over to Elissa and said, "I love you!" To this day, I still haven't figured out how he was able to get out of his chair and walk without any help, let alone initiate a conversation by spontaneously saying "I love you!" Those few moments were a miracle of sorts, and an incredible adrenaline rush for everyone who witnessed them. It showed how much they loved their grandchildren and how the mind can sometimes overcome the body's limitations.

When Sienna was born on March 3, 2016, my mother was thrilled for all of us and overjoyed that she was able to see the birth of her great-granddaughter. My father didn't understand what it all meant by then, but he always loved children and very much enjoyed having the baby around. In fact, in *shul,* the kids would come up to him because they knew he had lollipops or candy for them in his *tallis* bag.

Unfortunately, his Alzheimer's had robbed him of the light he shined on us with his smile and good humor. Too often, he was in his own world with a blank look. Despite the progression of the disease, however, he never forgot my mother or her name.

Finally, the following January, he passed away after a trip to the hospital because he was having difficulty breathing. It was a devastating loss for all of us. My mother had great difficulty dealing with the situation while he was in hospice care at home and then when he died. Having Brenda, Sue and me around, as well as her grandchildren, helped her to go on.

Helping, too, was the fact that Elissa became pregnant. When she found out, she couldn't wait to tell my mother, and she made her promise she would live to see her baby. It was important to both of them. As I noted, my mother made goals and the new goal was to see Elissa's baby. She said she wanted "to meet" her baby.

When Zachary William Halperin was born on October 17, 2017, my mother rejoiced in the news and then immediately looked forward to the *bris* since Zachy was going to be named after my father, who had passed away nine months earlier. It was as if my father's soul would carry on in Zachy. My mother was so happy at his *bris*, and everyone was happy for her, watching as she held her new great-grandson. She had kept her promise to Elissa—she was there for her and for Zachy.

My mother had privately told Eric, at Sienna's first birthday party: "He should be here." She was referring to my father. She loved hearing about and seeing Sienna and Zachy. She couldn't stop talking about how beautiful they were. Elissa and Eric would call her, but the conversations did not last very long because my mother's pain kept her from being as gregarious as she had once been. Once she learned over the phone that everybody was doing well and was healthy, she was happy.

Several months after Zachy's birth, my mother passed away suddenly, on Mother's Day of 2018. We were all going to see her later in the day, but I got a call early that morning from Julie, her aide, that something was wrong.

I drove over and called the hospice team, but the doctor did not respond. I gave her something to drink and some apple sauce to settle her nausea, and she thanked me. She said she loved me and lay down to sleep some more, and it seemed as if things would be OK. I told Sue and Brenda they didn't have to come because we would see her later that day.

Then Julie called out to me from the bedroom and said she didn't think she was alive. When I checked, she was gone. Towards the end, when people were telling her to drink or eat and she was not up to it, she would say in no uncertain terms, "Leave me alone. I just want to be with my husband." On May 13, 2018, she got her wish and joined my father. They both died in their home, which is what they wanted. The losses are still felt deeply. At the same time, I am grateful I could see them really enjoy their family and friends, especially when Elissa, Eric and later Sammy were in their lives. I feel lucky I had them around until I was 67 years old, and they were able to enjoy their grandchildren for over 37 years. Elissa and Eric were able to see them as they were before the diseases began to erode their resilience and warmth and vitality. It is too bad my mother could not meet Ruby Eve Farkas and Zoe Esther Halperin, her great-granddaughters, who were born after she died and were named after her. Ruby's Hebrew name is Esther, and Zoe's is Esther Liba. I hope they have her strength and embrace life the way she did.

Having grandchildren, and being with them, is the greatest joy

Sue and I could possibly have. We were lucky to have taken care of Sienna and Zachy one day a week apiece and to watch them grow and develop. I wish we could do that with Ruby and Zoe, but my cancer and Covid make that impossible. Still, we have watched all four of them grow and become their own unique personalities and have also seen how much our children get a kick out of their children and what great parents they are. All of this warms our hearts, and we have so much love when we are all together. It is hard to believe Sue and I are the eldest generation now. But we are, and we proudly wear our titles of Zeide and Grammy. We are truly blessed.

11

LESSONS LEARNED

MY PARENTS WERE NOT the most religious people to survive the Holocaust. And others, for sure, were more intellectually gifted or more altruistic. They always felt it was pure luck that they had made it out alive when others hadn't, but their survival suggests they had qualities and strengths that enabled them to endure the terror and murderous brutality of the Holocaust and then go on to lead meaningful lives afterward.

My father, grandfather and Uncle Moishe experienced a period of daily horrors that was designed to ultimately kill them and yet they found a way to live. My mother, at a young age, was separated from her parents and tasked with the responsibility of taking care of her younger siblings in an uncertain setting with a different religion, culture and language. She never knew whether she and her siblings would be reunited with their parents. Nevertheless, she did what she had to do to make sure she and they could get through each day. Their fortitude, strength, resilience and courage cannot be denied and, in fact, should be honored and never forgotten. I have chosen 10 lessons I learned from them, which I believe are worthy of being passed along to all who read this book.

1. Have faith that things will work out and
2. Do not be afraid to take risks

This amounts to really being optimistic and not being intimidated by difficult circumstances.

Throughout the war, my father took risks by volunteering for jobs he was not qualified for so that, perhaps, he would have the opportunity to get something for himself and his brother that would help them survive. My parents took a risk by coming to another country—the United States—with a different language and very little money, all in hopes of starting a new life, becoming citizens and owning a house and a business. In William Helmreich's book *Against All Odds*, he quotes Rabbi Shlomo Riskin, who said: "What makes Jews remarkable is not that they believe in God after Auschwitz, but that they have children after Auschwitz. That they affirm life and a future." This was always true in my family. My parents always believed that they and we, as their children, would make it all work out. I say this to my children often as well. It does not mean ignoring what is going on. Surely you must do what you can to address a problem or a goal. However, it is also important to believe in yourself enough, and to have faith that you will figure it out and things will work out in the end. No matter what the result, you will have grown from the experience.

My father had always wanted his own store and my mother her

own house. While my father had his own business in Belgium, he had to do it in secret because non-citizens could not own a business there. It took him until the early 1960s to finally have his own store in Rego Park, Queens. That is almost 20 years after the war ended. My mother finally got her house in 1967. However, it took several years for them to furnish this house the way she wanted. She would buy one item (like a coffee table) at a time until the room was done. She had goals right through to the last part of her life, when she wanted to dance at a grandchild's wedding or to see her great-grandchildren be born. She pursued these goals with the idea that it would work out and be achieved. And it did work out.

I believe my career as a school and clinical psychologist occurred only because I dared to substitute for an absent reading teacher at the Adams School when I went to look for a job as a social studies teacher. I knew nothing about teaching reading or, really, anything at all about special education. I relied only on my gut instincts and the belief I could do it. That decision led to me becoming the permanent substitute and then having my own class. I also met and worked with two of the best school psychologists I ever knew.

I had no idea there was such a job until then. I was ready to become a special education teacher and was 18 credits into my Masters program when a pink slip from the New York City Board of Education led me to go back to school for my masters degree and certification in school psychology. Again, it was a risk, but it all worked out and I believe, as I have said many times, I ended up doing what I was meant to do. Be bold, and dare to take a risk when the opportunity presents itself. It is by taking chances that we learn that we can be brave and grow. This is not unlike a child learning to walk. He or she will often stumble and fall. Yet it is the trying and falling that leads to the successful walking and then running.

3. Family and Friends Are Most Important

My mother always insisted that losing so much of her family during the Holocaust made maintaining a family the most important thing in life. Furthermore, because my mother and father came from large families that had shrunk to a precious few, friends became like family after the war. Since the time I was young, we always had some family members living with us—Uncle Moishe, when he first came to the United States; my maternal grandmother for over 25 years; and my paternal grandfather for several years when he was contemplating moving to the United States in the mid 1980s. My parents also had a lot of friends who would socialize regularly in one another's homes. All of our holidays included family and friends at my parents' home. Thankfully, Sue and I have continued that tradition. Unlike the days of the *shtetl*, where everybody knew everybody else and family and friends were very close by, now our friends and family are all over the country and world. We have worked hard to bridge those gaps in geography. As I get older, I realize the need to stay in close touch with people who knew us when we were young and with whom we have a shared history. So, nurture these relationships with family, friends, co-workers and colleagues. It is vital.

As Barbara Bush, the former First Lady, once said: "When the dust settles and all the crowds are gone, the things that matter most are faith, family and friends." I could not agree more with this sentiment. Someone once said: "It is not what we have in life that is important, but who we have in life that really matters." I have been lucky, in my life, to have my parents, my children, my family and friends and especially Sue. Sue is my wife, my best friend and the love of my life. Words can hardly describe what she means to me. Now I have four loving and wonderful grandchildren as well.

4. Live in the Present

My parents did not talk to us about the Holocaust and the enormous suffering and loss they had endured until we were much older. They only spoke about it when we asked and when they were interviewed for the Shoah Foundation project. They very much lived in the present while also having goals for the future. As we were growing up, they worked hard to achieve those goals and often did not enjoy what was going on as much as they could have, but they never dwelt on the past. They got better at enjoying the present once they were older and had grandchildren. Sue and I had goals, but we very much lived in the present, enjoying our children and our lives, as it was occurring. Don't let life slip away by living in the past or worrying about the future. By living your life one day at a time, you live all the days of your life. There is a saying, "Yesterday is history. Tomorrow is a mystery. Today is a gift. That's why they call it the present." In addition, don't rush things by wishing this stage or this phase was over. Live in the moment, and enjoy the ride, bumps and all. Since I learned about my cancer, I do not worry about the future. I am taking care of all that is in my control and I am confident it will work out. I live one day at a time, but I am playing the long game.

5. Focus on What You Have and Not on What You Don't

My parents were never jealous of others or what others had. They focused on what they wanted and what they had. They worked towards getting and achieving their goals, but as long as everyone was fine and healthy, they were happy. Elissa and Eric used to say that conversations with my mother were fairly short because once she knew you were fine, she was fine. I have lived my life the same way. Having things and a lot of money was not so important to me. My kids teased me when they wanted to get me a present for my birthday or Father's Day because when asked what I needed or wanted, I would often say, "Nothing." Clearly, having things and money is better than not having it. Sue and I have been quite fortunate to have way more creature comforts than we ever dreamed of—but we realize what is most important is health, family, and friends to share good times with. When you focus on what you have, work towards your goals and have faith you will get what you want, you will rid yourself of bad feelings that result from focusing on what you do not have. It is the old maxim of the glass half full or half empty. Those who are optimistic and have faith see the glass as half full, and those who are pessimistic see it as half empty. I thoroughly adhere to the saying, "A rich person is not the one who has the most, but is the one that needs the least."

6. Be a Mensch...Do the Right Thing

My children know there is no greater praise from me than being a "*mensch*." That means being a good person. Life is about choices, and we are better when we make choices that emanate from kindness. I've learned people don't remember what you said or what you did, but they often remember how you made them feel. Thus, making someone else feel better when they are not in a good place, visiting a sick person and, in general, just doing the right thing when the opportunity arises, is a good way to live. Dr. Viktor Frankl, a psychiatrist and Holocaust survivor is a theorist I have always admired and use as a model to live my life and to help others. He stated that even in the concentration camps there were always choices. For example, do I share this piece of bread or eat it all myself? Every day and every minute there were choices to be made and decisions that determined whether you would give in to the Nazis' attempts to make you into something less than a human being and rob you of your inner freedom and dignity. Even when faced with death as the rifle was aimed at you, you had a choice as to how to act. Would you beg, cry, say a prayer (the *Shema*) or curse at your tormentors? Would you find a way to show strength?

I always told my children when they left the house--first as teenagers, and later as young adults—to make good decisions. I also told them that, in situations with all things being equal, if the choice is to do or to not do something, opt for doing it. You won't regret the things you do; you regret the ones you don't do. This includes small things like calling or visiting a sick friend, helping someone with directions when they are lost or calling your grandparent to say hello. Mother Teresa said, "The greatest good is what we do for one another." Similarly, Booker T. Washington once observed, "Those who are happiest are those who do the most for others." Don't think about it. Do it.

7. It Is Better To Give Than To Receive

As I noted, my parents' home was always welcoming, and if you came, you never left hungry, thirsty or not feeling good. Though we may have had issues with my mother, who could be tough, all our friends loved her and asked about my parents. I have written in this memoir of the ways my father gave jobs or time to people in the store just because. Neither of them did nice things or charitable things just to be noticed. In fact, I can recall that when we went to *shul* on Yom Kippur or other holidays, and the Kol Nidre appeal was conducted and the donations from members of the congregation announced, my father would not hand in the paper or card stating how much he was giving. Instead, he preferred to wait until after the holiday, so that his donation was anonymous. He always gave anonymously. All this goes with being a mensch.

Mahatma Gandhi said, "The simplest acts of kindness are by far more powerful than a thousand heads lowering in prayer." When you help someone else, when you do something for them, you will feel better. I often talk with patients who are depressed or feel hopeless and tell them to think of a person they can help or ways they can make others feel better. Doing this often lifts their spirits and makes them feel better. The quickest way to receive love and feel good about yourself is to give love to others.

8. Always Do Your Best

I saw my father and mother commit to their jobs. They took pride in what they did. My father was a tailor and always did his best and worked hard, not just to eventually get his own business but to do right by his customer and by his standards. I can recall an incident when he left his car on Main Street in Queens, near our house, because the roads were so icy everyone was skidding out of control. He felt he could not drive to his store, so he left the car there. He then walked well over a mile on a slippery, icy street to the train station, and then another mile to the store, because he was committed to being there for his job. He later called me to retrieve the car. Sue's dad, also a tailor, walked over the 59th Street Bridge to get to his job in Sutton Place in Manhattan from his house in Astoria when the trains weren't running due to a transit strike. My mother was the same. No matter the job, no matter what you're being asked to do, commit and do your best. I put in extra time when I needed to so I could do my best. I never regretted it, no matter the result. I felt great when I knew I did my best and nothing was said as opposed to people lauding what I did when I felt it was not so terrific. As in almost anything, as you do it, you will get better at it. If you do your best all the time, you will hasten growth to the point where you will be able to figure out most things fairly easily. To prove how much my father identified as a tailor, I saw him in his later years when he had Alzheimer's and couldn't recall my name. I would take him to go see a doctor and after the visit, he would say to the doctor, "Tell me your size, I'll make you a suit." It was his way of thanking the doctor, of saying, if only he still could: "You gave me your best, I'll give you my best." Pablo Picasso once said, "The meaning of life is to find your gift. The purpose of life is to give it away."

9. Act with Humility

The question one should always ask is: How do I take pride in what I do and stay humble at the same time? However, I do not think it is that hard. As C.S. Lewis put it, "Humility is not thinking less of yourself, it is thinking of yourself less." It is about doing the job with pride but thinking about the person who will benefit from your job or work and not about yourself. When you are taking pride in your work, you are not thinking about yourself but throwing yourself totally into it for the person for whom you are doing it. When that occurs, it is therapeutic and a liberating experience, since you are not at all self-absorbed but, instead, one with the task at hand. That is how I felt when I made the collages or paintings for my children or anyone. It was not done for money or anything other than giving it away.

In my work as a school psychologist, I almost always gave the credit to the staff and to the parents. As a therapist, the credit goes to the patient, as it is the patient who is doing the work and I am there for the patient.

Again, it is better to give to others than receive or look to receive credit for what you do. As was noted earlier, you know when you are doing something well and the good feeling that results comes from within and not from others. Saying "thank you" is the simplest and often the best example of humility because you are thinking about the other person. When we think of others with an open and loving heart, we are our best versions of ourselves.

I hardly ever spoke about my work as a school psychologist, clinical psychologist or college professor or supervisor. I was asked to apply to be a Diplomate—a recognition that you are among the best in your field—and decided not to because I didn't believe in outsiders judging whether I was or was not good enough to be a Diplomate. I believed my work was between me and the people I worked with. As it turned out, without my permission, one of my psychologist interns and my school principal (Steve Furrey) nominated me for Nassau County School Psychologist of the Year. I was fortunate enough to win this prestigious honor, and my family, including my parents, were in attendance at the award ceremony. I thanked all the people who enabled me to be the psychologist I am, including the staff I worked with who allowed me to work the way I saw fit.

Everyone at the school came to the ceremony, as did many previous psychologist interns I had trained. My parents were impressed by the award and of course told me how proud they were. At my retirement from Central Boulevard School, many people got up and talked about how I had helped them and what I meant to them, including Steve Furrey, who got choked up when he spoke. Afterwards, my father came up to me and said, "I never knew you did all this." I was happy, not because he realized after 40 years what I did, but because, like him, I did my work without fanfare. I just did my best and always tried to do the right thing.

10. Remember and Respect Those Who Came Before You

It's important to know and honor those who came before and paved the road you walk on. Our job on this journey through life on this Earth is to make some impact and contribute in somehow making the world a better place. Many, if not most, succeed in ways to make it better. As a parent I hope my children will do better than me. My parents wanted Eddie, Brenda and me to do better than they did and to have an easier time than they did. I believe they, as well as Sue and I, succeeded.

However, it was the things they did that enabled us to accomplish what we did. They came to the United States with little money, spoke another language and had to learn how to maneuver through life in a big city after growing up in a small *shtetl* where nobody went to college and very few had a profession. What we have, we owe to them and those who came before them. That is true not just for family but for others who came before us. We drive around easily because some people literally paved the road we walk and drive on. We rarely think about that, but it is true. Many, many people contributed to make things better for us in big and small ways.

Jacob Riis, the social activist, observed, "When nothing seems to help, I go look at a stonecutter hammering away at his rock perhaps a hundred times without as much as a crack showing in it. Yet at the hundred and first blow, it will split in two, and I know it was not that blow that did it, but all that had gone before." I used to tell teachers, especially special education teachers who did not feel their work showed how much the student had learned, that sometimes we do not see the results of our work. Sometimes, it is the next teacher who sees that child finally get it and, hopefully, realizes everything that went before that enabled that child to finally understand what was being taught. I realize what came before impacts us in the present and the future. An example, unfortunately, is the environment. What we do now will affect the future of our planet and how future generations live.

I hope you will see that these 10 lessons are very much intertwined. I hope they serve you well.

In addition, I suggest you find meaning and purpose in your life. It will help tremendously in difficult moments and it will inspire you. Most important, it will bring you joy. My parents' meaning came from a decision to go forward and start a family. In addition, they were determined to pursue their dreams and live with optimism and the idea that they would achieve their dreams. I am so proud to see that they did.

CODA

THE FAMILY AND FAMILY FRIENDS (almost all Holocaust survivors) I grew up knowing are almost all gone. My grandparents, my parents, Uncle Benny and Uncle Moishe have passed on. Even my brother, Eddie, has passed away, succumbing to Covid on March 29, 2020. As the Holocaust survivors leave us, it is our duty to remember (*Zachor*) all of them, and especially the ones who didn't survive at the time. We need to tell our children, and they need to tell their children, the story of their ancestors and the Holocaust, so that they can impart the lessons learned. The Fifth Commandment stipulates the Jewish obligation of memory. "Honor Your Father and Mother" refers to the commitment of all Jews to honor those who came before them. Some of them were brave survivors who suffered from and were witness to the atrocities of hate and genocide. We, in turn, must be watchful of the evil that still lives in the ideologies of hatred and prejudice.

It is my fervent wish that this book enables my children and grandchildren and future generations to know and to be proud of their heritage. I want them to know they had ancestors who had so much taken from them and were treated inhumanely during the Holocaust. However, once they were liberated and dealt with the tremendous losses of their families, their own youth, their health and so much more, they chose to live again, to love again, to trust again and to be happy again. I want my children, grandchildren and the next generations to realize they have Farkas blood running through their veins and that it carries love, inner strength and fortitude. I hope it serves all of you well.

With all my love,

Your Zeide
Ervi (Heshy) Farkas

Appendices

APPENDIX A
Map of Ukraine

Map of Transcarpathia

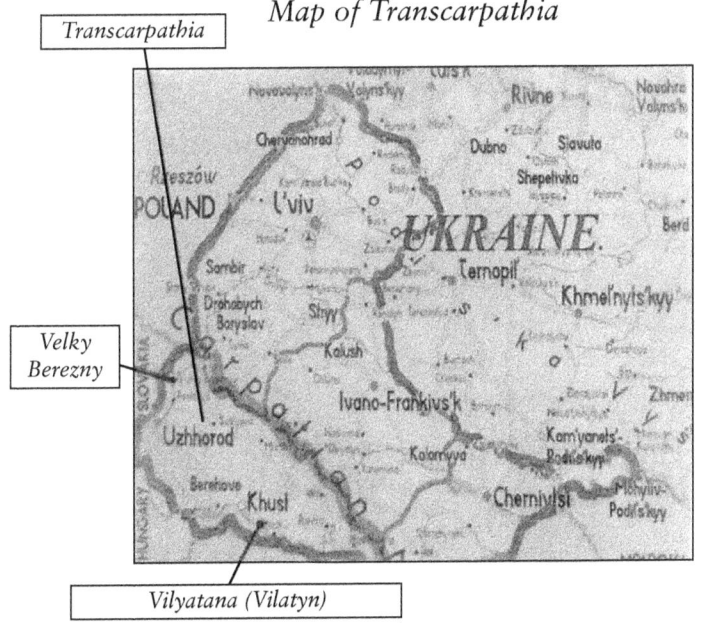

APPENDIX B: FARKAS FAMILY TREE

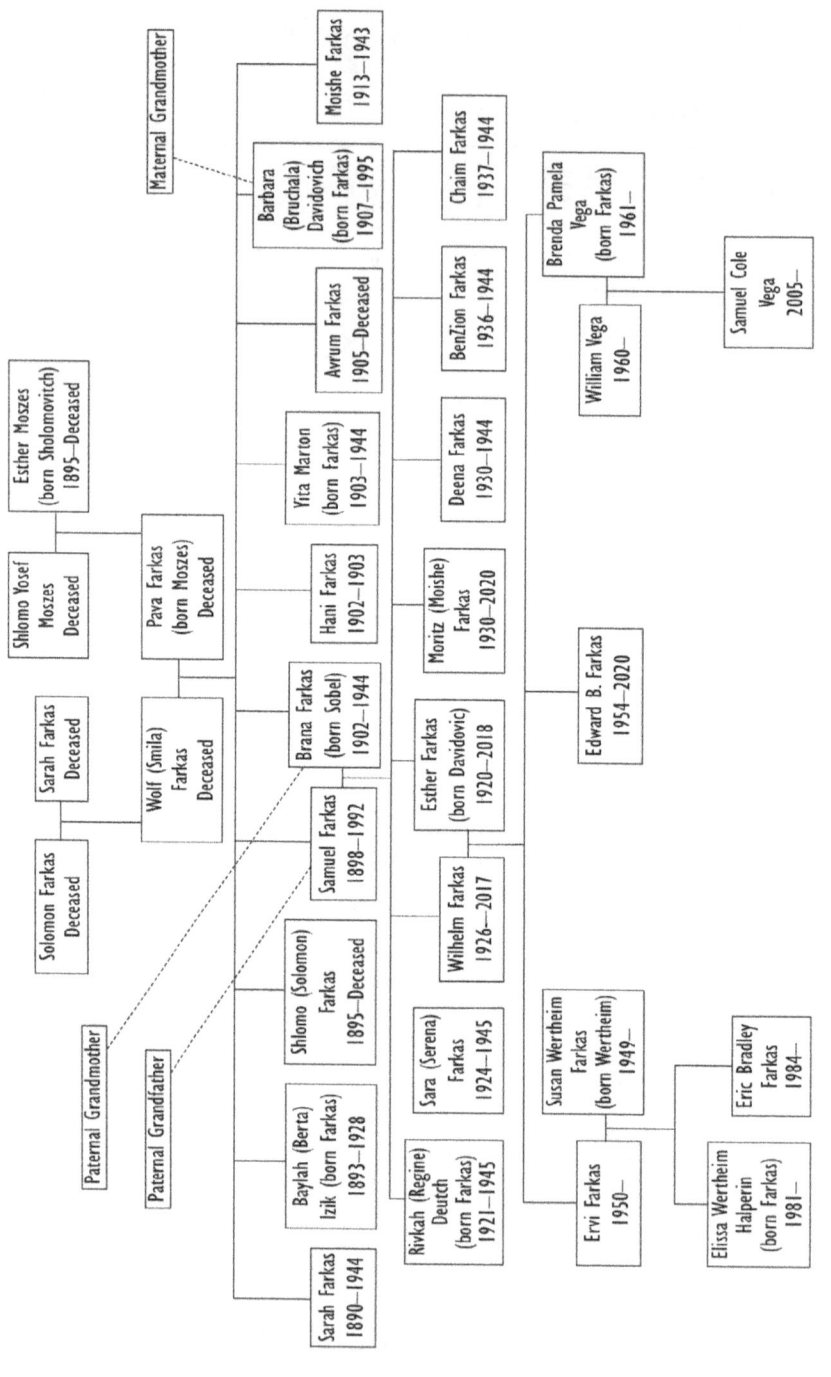

APPENDIX C: SOBEL FAMILY TREE

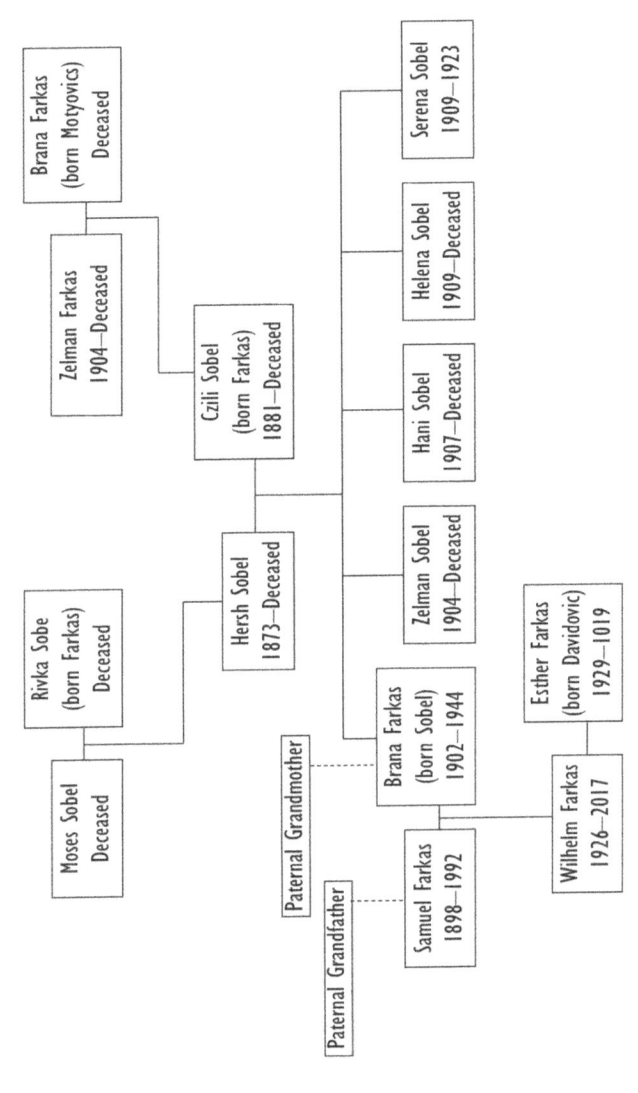

APPENDIX D: DAVIDOVIC FAMILY TREE

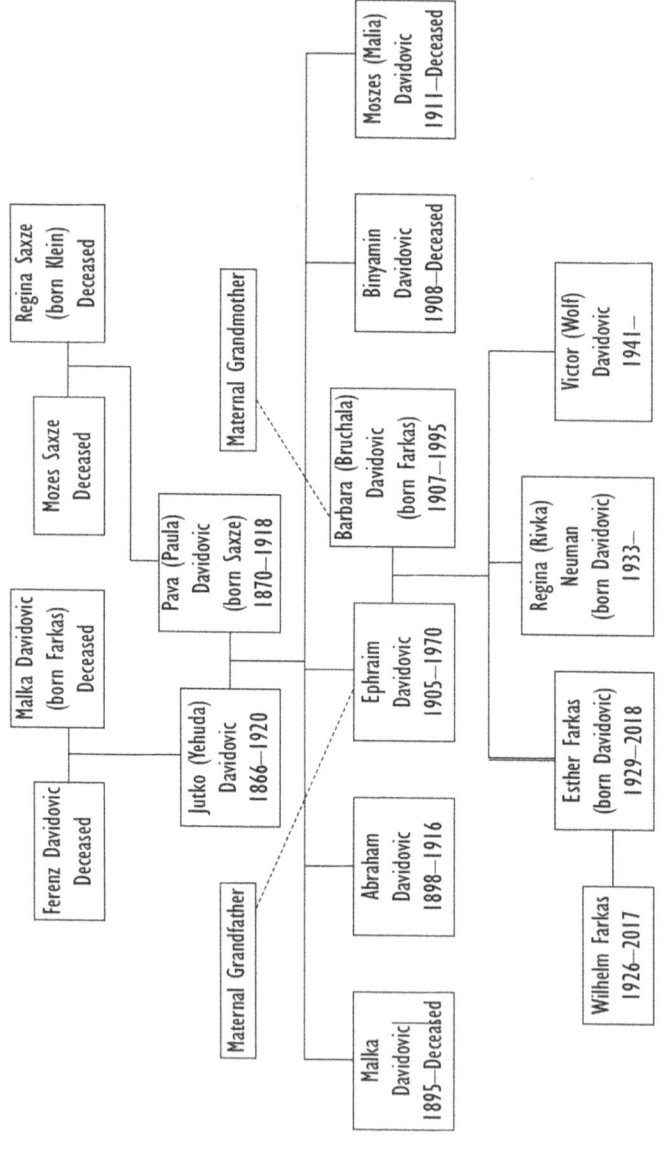

APPENDIX E

Eulogies for My Father, Wilhelm Farkas

Erv's Eulogy

First of all, on behalf of our family, I would like to thank all of you for coming here today.

I want to tell you a little bit about my father and what he meant to us. My brother, Eddie, will share some anecdotes that will highlight what I am about to say. Growing up with two parents who survived the Holocaust, I always felt that event, which occurred before I was born, influenced me and affected who I and my brother and sister are and how we behave. However, I can not swear to you that the Holocaust had the same effect on my dad.

Of course, I know it had profound effects on him. How could it not, when you are a young teenager and your family is taken out of its home and herded into a crowded ghetto room where there is very little in the way of such comforts as food or a comfortable bed. Since my grandfather was working in the forests of the Carpathian Mountains at the time the family was taken to the ghetto, my father, at 15, was the eldest male and felt a duty to find ways to provide what he could for his family. That meant volunteering for whatever work details there were so he could possibly find some food and other things to bring back for the family.

Later towards the end of the war, the last year, they were taken to Auschwitz, where he was branded A-11030; his brother, Uncle Moishe, was A-11029. Through sheer determination, guile and a whole lotta luck, he and Uncle Moishe survived, as did my grandfather. His five siblings and mother did not survive, along with countless extended family. My uncle Moishe called me when he learned my father was in hospice care and he cried how he was not only losing a brother but that my father was like a mother and father to him.

Coming to the U.S. was not easy either. My parents left my mother's family in Belgium, where they had met and married. I was born a little over a year later. My father became a tailor. He did well until the Korean War, and then all businesses suffered. So they emigrated to the U.S. with a little over $80.00 in his pocket. There were a few months in Texas, and then we settled in Williamsburg, Brooklyn, where there was some family. I was now 3 1/2 years old. My brother, Eddie, was born shortly afterwards. We all slept in one room. I recall the stories of how my father, without speaking English beyond a few words, figured out the subway system and got a job in the Garment Center in Manhattan and then a second job near our apartment in Williamsburg, where he worked in the evenings and on Sundays—all within two days of being in New York.

Growing up, I don't recall my father ever throwing a ball around with us or, later on, seeing me play baseball or basketball. The only day we had with my father was Shabbos. And on Shabbos we went to shul in the morning, came home and ate, and my father invariably took a nap. Later, he was up and we went to shul again. We had very little, and we were probably poor but we never felt poor—even when my brother, sister and I slept together in a room that had suits and other clothing hanging over our heads because our father was trying to start his own business and eventually buy a store, which he did. We didn't feel poor because everyone else we knew was in fairly similar circumstances. We had family and friends who were all survivors and trying to build new lives for themselves and their families.

I cannot recall man-to-man talks with my dad growing up. He was not a big talker. He was a doer. He worked to provide for us, make us feel safe and had a strong work ethic and pride in his craft. His humanity taught us the values we now live with. After my father bought the store and he did well, we moved to Queens and bought a home there. The house was around the corner from his best friend, Joe, whom he had reunited with years after the war and well after we came to New York.

Despite the degradation and dehumanization during the war and the struggles afterwards, my father never lost his dignity and his humanity. He loved being around people and especially family and friends. As my mother once said to us, when you lose so much family as they did, friends become so much more important. My parents always welcomed our friends to the house, and our house was the place for most holidays and celebrations. We grew up with the idea, if someone doesn't have a seder or a meal to eat, you invite them over. Sue and I have continued that tradition at our house.

When I was older and worked in my father's store with him, he always had older people coming in to sit and chat for a while. He always talked with them as he worked and let them stay as long as they wanted. He had an elderly man, Mr. Mendelson, who was retired from the milk wagon business, so I have no idea how old he was because at that time, I thought 30 was old. Mr. Mendelson came every day, sometimes before my father opened the store, so he could do an occasional delivery and sweep the floors. My father, who did not go past sixth grade in cheder due to the war, spoke five or six languages so he spoke to just about anyone in their native tongue. Once, I saw him talking to a Chinese man and I couldn't hear the conversation but it was animated. Later, I asked him how he was able to speak with him because he didn't speak Chinese. My father said, "He spoke to me in Chinese, and I answered him in Yiddish and we spoke." It was a joke, but he let me know it wasn't about the words, it was about conveying a sense of respect, a sense of caring.

Even when Alzheimer's robbed him of his cognitive skills and he didn't know who many of us were anymore, he still had that giving and loving personality. We would go to the neurologist and although he couldn't answer any of the questions asked, afterwards he would say to the doctor: "I'm a tailor— tell me your size, and I'll make you a suit." The last few years, when I would come to shower him, with Julie, his aide, he would fight as he hated water on him and it would be a 20-minute struggle with kicking and grabbing. However, once it was over and we gave him a towel, he would say "Thank you, thank you." So, the Holocaust did not define him or change who he was in terms of his loving and giving soul.

I used to tell my kids that Zeide was a better grandfather than a father because he had time with and for them that he didn't have when we were growing up. He loved children and especially his grandchildren and now Sienna, his great-granddaughter. He always had candies in his tallis bag for the kids in shul. Nothing gave him more joy than being surrounded by Elissa, Eric and Sammy. He would laugh with them, play with them and even threw a ball around with them.

My father was also devoted to my mother. He once said he fell in love with her from the moment he saw her. That love never wavered and in fact, she was the only one he still recognized and knew as Alzheimer's was destroying his brain. One time, my mom was in the hospital and we went to take him to see her. He was already not recognizing members of our family and his skills were declining. He kept asking where she was and we would tell him she was in the hospital. He would ask again and he would look out the window for her. When we got to her room, he saw her and immediately walked over to her and said, "Here you are. I was missing you." Brenda, Sue and I started crying. Last week was their 68th wedding anniversary.

To Elissa, Eric, Sammy and Sienna. . .always know you are part of an incredibly strong, resilient and loving legacy.

Before I end, I want to relay a story I recalled a few days ago. My dad, as I said, didn't talk much about himself and he certainly never bragged. But he did talk up his friends, like Joe or his brother and especially his father. He would tell us how his father was so smart and "gelearent," meaning he had learned a lot. He spoke about how his father was a poet who wrote Purim Spiels for the town and everybody in the shtetl couldn't wait to see what he wrote about them. He bragged how his father was the manager of the workers in the forest who chopped down trees and, because of that, was away from home. When I was 8 years old, my mother, Eddie and I went to Belgium to visit my mother's family—Babi and Zeide and Uncle Victor. After a week, we went to Metz, France, to visit my father's father—Der Zeide as my father called him—and his second wife. I'm thinking to myself how I can't wait to meet this guy who my father talked up as the smartest guy—a poet and a woodsman. I'm expecting someone who looks like Paul Bunyan, tall with muscles, etc., and as they are walking towards us, here is a 5-foot-5 small man with a yarmulke that covered his whole head. To my father, this little man was a giant.

Dad, you were a giant, and we have learned the lessons well. I love you. You are in all of us and I think I may have become you.

Eddie's Eulogy

One day it was my turn to open my dad's shop and take care of it while he went into the city to get fabrics and other supplies for customers. In walked a nun with flowers. She asked if Willy was in. I said he was getting some fabrics, how could I help? She asked if I could give him the flowers. I inquired if I could ask why, and she explained that he, for years, helped out with clothes for the children of the orphanage. . . . That was Willy, helping and not talking about it, helping, no matter religion, color, age. That was Willy.

In shul, a neurologically challenged boy greeted him. His clothes were crooked and too large for his frame. My dad smiled, put his arm on his shoulder and warmly asked him to come to his house, which he did, so he could fix him a nice suit for services. Neither one ever thought about charging—it was a gift each was giving to the other. That was Willy.

When I was younger, I noticed he had assistants in the store. I never understood why such a humble shop needed assistants. It turns out he knew that these older men needed the dignity of feeling useful, so he gave them a few dollars a day to sweep, run errands, so they felt they had a job, were still useful and despite their very advanced age were important. He did that even when the business was slow—he made them feel important. That was Willy.

He also had a dry sense of humor. When I was a child, I was amazed that he knew how to drive from Brooklyn to Queens or Brooklyn to Long Island. I asked him how he knew all that. It seemed to me, as a child, amazing. He confided to me that actually, he had no idea. He really didn't know. It was the car. In fact, he would show me. We went from Brooklyn to Queens and he told me to look at the dashboard very carefully. He pointed out that on the dashboard there was a signal blinking to turn left and he said: "See the car is telling me it's time to turn." The car knows the way. That was Willy.

When his Alzheimer's was advanced but there were still brief moments of lucidity, I got him to take a walk with me. During the walk he said, "I'm afraid."

I asked him, "What are you afraid of?"

"I might get lost. . .and if I get lost. . .Esther will be all alone," he replied.

Warmth, generosity, humor, caring, love.   That was Willy. I am so proud he was my father.

Sue's Eulogy

Hi. I'm Sue. I know I speak for everyone in saying we are just so sad. For the past 42 years, Zeide—as we called him—was like a father to me. I married Erv when Zeide was 48 and Grandma was 45. He died yesterday at 90 years of age. He was married to his beloved Esther for 68 years.

Zeide was an extraordinary man. He touched so many lives and because he was so humble and unassuming, one didn't always know the impact he had. People who met him once or twice said in recent days, "What a nice man," or, "His smile and cute personality brightened the room." Another friend, Babs, described his strength and humanity throughout his life.

It is a testimony to Zeide that Terry, the daughter of his best and lifelong friend, Joe, was so devoted to him that she flew in from Los Angeles to be with him at this time. She considered him a second father. His nieces and nephews were always there to be with him also.

His grandchildren adored him and gave him the utmost joy. His children gave him everything he so richly deserved. In sickness and health, they were by his side. They could not have done more. Their love, devotion and care made his brightest days brighter and his bleakest days easier. They tended to him over the long stretch of his illness until his dying days with tremendous love and respect, looking out for his physical needs, managing countless jobs, big and small, giving him comfort, and always telling him in word and deed, how much they loved him.

And Esther, "Grandma" as we called her, loved him and was always literally by his side. They built a life together and had many wonderful times. As Grandma says, it was always about family being together, and if we were good, they were good. When they had to deal with loss and sickness, they got through this, too, as with everything else, together. At each other's side. With support and trust and love.

Zeide opened up his heart to all of us and, in his final days, family and friends who loved him his whole life were there. The most beautiful, perfect sendoff, and it was befitting for the fine husband, father, Zeide, brother, uncle and friend he was.

Zeide and Grandma created a home that for years was where we spent all the holidays. We have the best and richest memories. It was a blessing that they were able to be at Lissy and Eric's bat and bar mitzvahs and weddings, to have sweet Sammy, and to live to see their precious great-granddaughter Sienna's birth.

I am blessed to have this family. From day one, Zeide and Grandma always made me feel so much a part of the family. The first time I met them was on Grandma and Zeide's 25th wedding anniversary. They were both so warm and inviting. They would say I was more a daughter, not a daughter-in-law. Zeide would tease and laugh with me. I nicknamed us the Farks; he liked that and would always repeat it as "the Foxes." When we arrived for the holidays with several bags, he'd always ask if we were staying for a month. He loved my chocolate nut cake and I would send it to them, even in Florida. He was so kind to my parents, talking tailor talk with my dad: "How much do you charge for cuffs? . . . Where do you buy your trimmings?" They were 20 years apart in age, but always sharing an easy rapport and mutual respect and love.

Zeide was a very observant Jew. He would come to shul with me when I said Kaddish for my parents. He even said Kaddish for several friends/family who had no one else to say it. That's the kind of man he was. And now, my wonderful husband, his Heshy, will in death give him the greatest respect, just as he did in life.

I thank all of you for giving us so much love and support. We are eternally grateful.

I love you, Zeide. May you rest in peace.

Elissa's Eulogy

My name's Elissa—or Lissy to my Zeide. I was his first grandchild and probably his favorite. At least that's what I like to think. But even if it was not true, I know without a doubt that my grandfather loved me and I loved him.

I used to love to sleep over at Grandma and Zeide's when I was kid—mostly because they would always keep their house stocked with Trix and other sugary cereals that my parents wouldn't let us have in our house—but also because Grandma and Zeide were such amazing grandparents and went out of their way to make sure my brother and I were happy, comfortable, cared for and having fun.

And whether we were spending a weekend with them in Queens or a week in Florida, we always were happy, comfortable, cared for and having fun. We were lucky. We had great grandparents. And we still have an amazing grandmother whose devotion to her husband for the past 68 years is truly remarkable.

But today, I just want to share a couple of stories that I will always keep close to my heart and that I think really show the kind of grandfather that Zeide was.

When I was young, I would go to temple with Zeide and I enjoyed sitting on the rabbi's lap and always knew that at some point Zeide would surprise me by pulling a lollipop out of his pocket and giving it to me. But the moment when Zeide truly was my hero was one Rosh Hashanah, when we were walking to the water to throw away our sins and we passed a store that was selling the new Teen Beat magazine and my dad told me that I couldn't get it because you can't spend money on the High Holy Days. A block later, my Zeide surprised me with the magazine, and I was so happy. I remember that my favorite actor at the time was on the cover, and I really wanted it. I found out later that Zeide knew the store owner and told him he would come back the next day to pay him for the magazine. He did that without even breaking the rules of the High Holy Days—just in case anyone was worried. He wanted me to be happy and found a way to make that day special.

Twenty five years later, I found the actual man of my dreams and not whoever was on the cover of that magazine, and even though a lot has changed, my Zeide still found a way to make the happiest day of my life even more special by giving me a gift that I will always be grateful for. Having him and my grandma attend my wedding to my husband Ben was so important to me—but Zeide was suffering from Alzheimer's disease and having him walk down the aisle and say the blessing over the challah were not guaranteed. It was hard to know if he would even recognize me, let alone cooperate with our other plans for him that day. But my Zeide came through for me. He walked down the aisle—stopping on the way to shake people's hands, I'm told—and then he said the Motzi, he danced the hora, and when he was leaving that night, he said, "I love you," to me. I knew in that moment how special that was and told both of my parents what had happened and how Zeide told me he loved me. It was the perfect wedding gift and something that I am eternally grateful for. I feel so lucky that my Zeide was able to see me marry the person that I love, and I will always keep his love in my heart and honor his memory in the years to come. I know my brother will share our Grandma and Zeide's stories with his daughter Sienna and I hope that my husband and I have the chance to pass it down to children and grandchildren of our own one day. And if I can one day make a child or grandchild as happy as my Zeide made me, I think I'll know that I did a good job.

I love you Zeide and will miss you.

Eric's Eulogy

Alta shmutziga momzer: Those three Yiddish words help define my relationship with my Zeide. What do they mean? I highly doubt anyone would guess it, but those three bonding words between a teenager and his grandpa mean: "old dirty bastard."

It was one of the many ways in which Zeide and I made each other laugh. Because he had a great sense of humor. And we had a special bond.

Long story long: I used to always imitate Zeide to find new ways to make him laugh. He was a fan of wearing his pants very high—like above-the-belly-button high. So I would joke around and do the same. I'd borrow his cap and put it on and hike my pants to my shoulders and we'd all laugh. Him, too.

ASM/ODB was funny because he and the rest of the adults would speak Yiddish. I'd have no idea what they were saying and it all sounded the same to me. So I'd imitate them and they'd yell at me. I surprised them all by learning three real words—my French teacher had a weird sense of humor, and that's what she taught me. Zeide thought it was hilarious. We all did.

Zeide lost a piece of himself as he got older, but I'm not going to focus on that. Now is a time to celebrate his life. It's a time to wash away some of the recent memories and focus on a life well-lived.

Holocaust survivor

Farkas family patriarch. Built the Farkas brand in the U.S.

Father of three—four if you count my mom, who has been like a daughter to them for over 40 years

Grandfather of 3—including seeing my sister marry Ben and me marry my loving, supportive wife, Jess

Great-grandfather of one

Married for 68 years

"Wintered" in Florida. "Summered" in Queens.

Dedicated himself to God to help my Grandma beat cancer

Entrepreneur

Small business owner

Gardener in his spare time

Frequent giver of candy to kids about to lose their minds at temple

Not afraid to pound on the table during a seder to keep people on task or yell at me for playing under the table.

That's a helluva life. When you look back at his stats, he's a first-ballot Hall of Famer.

It's the first one that defined his life and my dad's life in some regards. Holocaust survivor is hard to understand. Two stories that I remembered that put in perspective how hard that must have been and how much of a warrior he was: (a) stolen bread; (b) goiter on neck saved life.

He lost his mom, two brothers, and all three of his sisters. He had his dad (my old Zeide) and his bro (Moishe) and got to it. Married my grandma, started a family, moved here, started a tailoring business and had a life well-lived.

He was an awesome Zeide. Bought me Trix cereal, took me to McD and Denny's, put up with all my nonsense and called me a chaya—loosely translated to wild thing.

As I got older, I went from playing under the table during meals to always wanting to sit next to him at the head of the table. I liked being close to him and learning from him.

Because of his big belly, he used to joke that he was pregnant and almost due. We would always joke and I'd ask him how many more months he had. It never got old. I'd make him laugh.

The circle of life is a sad, sobering, beautiful thing. The circle of life means Zeides become Old Zeides. Pretty special if you can become an Old Zeide. Means you got to span four generations. He deserved to be an old Zeide.

I know he didn't "know" Sienna and I know she won't remember him. But I've got pictures of the two of them together to prove it, and I sure hope their souls connected here. I trust they will connect in the future. Who she becomes remains to be seen, but based on what I know and feel, I think he and she would have gotten along well. Lots of smiles and laughs.

My Zeide is gone, but Sienna will have her own Zeide. I know that my Zeide taught her Zeide very well. She's in good hands. Like I was.

So let's remember to spend these next few days sharing stories and celebrating a life overcoming the worst of times. By fighting and turning it around and living a full life. I love you. I miss you. I'll see you again one day.

Sammy's Eulogy (11 years old)

Zeide was a great Zeide to me.

Although I didn't speak to him much because he didn't talk too much, there are many memories I have with him. I remember when I was very young, he and I would go into the garage in the Hamptons house and go into the car to play Yellow Submarine. He used to always give me candy, and what I really liked the most was when he gave me Häagen Dazs ice cream. I remember my mom telling me stories about Zeide in World War II, and how he would always volunteer to work because he was clever. Or that he ran a tailor shop after the war. When Zeide got sick on New Year's Eve, I thought he would get bette, and he did. It was just the next day after he got better, he got worse, and they took him to the hospital. I felt sad then. I miss him a lot already. I know that everyone who knew Zeide loved him and misses him because I know I loved him and miss him.

APPENDIX F

Eulogies for My Mother: Esther Farkas

Erv's Eulogy

First of all, on behalf of my family, I would like to thank all of you for coming today. I also want to thank some of the aides—Ndye, Indra, Hawa and especially Julie—who were there for my mother in more ways than you can imagine. To Julie, in particular, because you were there for so many years every night and most days and hardly took any days off.

I want to tell you a little bit about my mother and what she meant to us as a family. In the interest of all of you, I will try to keep it short as there are several speakers after me.

My mother was a friendly, outgoing, welcoming person who loved her family, her friends and our friends. In fact, she always asked about our friends as they did about her. All who met her liked or loved her. She was very independent and very much a person who took care of those around her.

As her cancer was progressing and her body was failing her, she became more frustrated and upset that she could not control her body and make it do what she wanted or not feel pain. As a result, she used to tell the aides fairly often how life for her was always hard and that she had to be in charge and take care of everybody and now she couldn't even take care of herself. It should be noted—she never talked about life being hard the first 80-plus years of her life because she was not a complainer. Even the day she died and was in agony when the hospice nurse asked her how she was, her initial response, half awake, was: "Comme ci, comme ca." She would recount to the aides how she had to leave Czechoslovakia and most of her family to move to Belgium and learn a new language when she started school there. Then, when the Germans marched into Belgium, it wasn't too long before all Jews had to wear the yellow star and things went from bad to worse.

When my mother was 12, my grandparents arranged with a neighbor to hide the three children in a convent/orphanage. All of a sudden, with very little preparation, my mother, along with my aunt Regine, who was 8, and my uncle Victor, who was 6 months old, were taken to the convent. They became Maria, Regine and Victor Jansen. My mother was told to watch out for her sister and brother and again learn a new language as the convent was in the Flemish-speaking part of Belgium. She, along with my aunt Regine, also had to learn how to be Catholics who knew the various prayers, as there were many recited several times a day in the convent. She had to learn to respond to a new name as well, so nobody would suspect they were Jews. My mother somehow got assigned to help with the little babies and toddlers, so she was able to look in on, and even feed, my uncle Victor and see that he was doing OK. They were there for almost four years while my grandparents were going from place to place, hiding themselves. Thankfully, they were among the lucky ones, as my grandparents came back to reclaim them.

It wasn't too long after that she met my father, and they married when she was 19. I was born a little over a year later. When I was 2, my parents left my mother's family in Belgium. Coming here with less than $80.00, they somehow, again, learned a new language and culture and were able to make a good life for themselves and the three of us. At different times my uncle Moishe lived with us, my grandmother (Babi) lived with us for 25 years and my grandfather (Old Zeide) stayed for over a year. My mom presided over all this, not to mention taking care of my dad his last years, when she was so sick herself. Our home was where the family gathered for many, many years for the seders and other family events. My mother was the balabusta, the person in charge. My dad may have had some veto power, but he rarely used it or was vetoed by my mother.

So her not being in charge and becoming more and more dependent on others was very difficult for her. She nevertheless remained friendly, welcoming and warm to all who came into her or our lives. She also never lost her sense of humor or her resilience in the face of adversity. For example, my cousin Moishe relayed a story when he called a few years ago and asked her how she was. She said, "Well, my husband has Alzheimer's, I have cancer but everything is good. It has to be."

As Moishe said, "That was inspiring."

My mother was a fighter and extremely determined. When things got really bad the last few years, she would make goals. She wanted to dance at Elissa's wedding, which she did, as she threw away her walker and danced the hora, as many of you remember. Then she wanted to be there for Sienna's birth and then Zachy's birth. She also used to say that she wanted to be there for Sammy's bar mitzvah, but she didn't think she would make it.

I think she fought the pain and her deteriorating body way longer than anyone else I know could have. In fact, I asked the oncologist at one point, a year ago, how long he thought she had left. He said he didn't know as he thought she should have probably been dead a year before.

I would like to believe she is with my dad now, as she said she wanted to be, and I know that is what my dad would want as well. But as I think about that, I tell myself, "Dad, your quiet times are coming to an end."

From my dad, I learned by example how to be a good person, to do the right thing and do the best that you can at your job. As I was writing this last night, I asked myself, "What did I learn from my mother?" And I remembered how she often said that family meant so much because they had lost so much family. She also said how important friends were because they had lost so much family and had many friends who had also lost family. So in the end, it doesn't matter how many languages you end up speaking, it is really about how you live your life and how you act with others.

Now that Grandma and Zeide are gone, as a family, we need to carry out the lessons taught as they lived their lives, as we only have each other. We also have to cherish our family and friends and appreciate, nurture and welcome our friends, as they are so important in our lives. To everyone here, I love you.

Mom, I love you.

Sue's Eulogy

Hi. I'm Sue. I know I speak for everyone in saying we are just so sad. The words of a Hebrew prayer keep coming to me. I feel a gaping hole. The universe feels different. Everything feels different because she touched our lives in such a profound way. My heart is heavy.

For the past 45 years, Grandma—as we called her—was a mother to me. I was the tender age of 24 when I met her. She was just so young at 44! So much was ahead of us. As the song goes, don't worry, I won't sing "Those Were The Days, My Friend."

Grandma, as you've heard, had a very full and rich life. She embraced life despite the hardships of her early and later years. She was ready to pick up and go, whether locally to friends and family, to plays, or travels to family in France, to Israel, to the Caribbean, and for years to Brenda's houses in the Hamptons and Miami Beach. She opened up her home to family and friends alike. But not just to her friends, to our friends as well and to her neighbors who had nowhere else to go. So many friends have been telling me about good conversations they had with her. She loved to tell her stories about her life.

Grandma loved having the family all around for the holidays. We would move in for days at a time when our kids were young so we could all celebrate the Jewish holidays together. Those are among my own kids' best memories. She made everyone feel very welcome. We thought it would go on always. And really, once she couldn't do it anymore, we were still always together at our house. Grandma always said it was about family being together, and that if we were good, she and Zeide were, too!

Grandma had many blessings, and her blessings were our blessings. She was a bride at 19, married to Zeide for 68 years, and loved him and was always by his side. They built a life together and enjoyed many wonderful times. She was a mom at 20, and she often said she grew up with her children. She was the matriarch in our family. Everyone who has seen the painting of her in their living room knows I'm not kidding! She was the big sister,,, and whether as a 12-year-old, when Aunt Regine was 8 and Uncle Victor was 6 months, or throughout the rest of her life, she was very devoted to them. She opened up her home and through the years, took care of Uncle Moishe, her mother and her father-in-law. She was feisty, she was strong, she was a fighter and she told it like she thought it.

Grandma was very appreciative for the love and attention we gave her. She would always say to me, "Enjoy," despite that she could no longer do what she once had. She said many times: "Look what becomes of a person." And despite the 26 years of battling her illness, she was, as the Hebrew prayer says, "granted the vigor" to live until 88 years of age.

She loved her grandchildren so much and took tremendous pleasure in them. She was extremely proud of Elissa, Eric and Sammy and always said they were such "good kids." She embraced Jess and Ben, and her warmth and love was showered on them as well. She could not have been more joyous to live to see them get married and to dance at their weddings. That will always fill my heart. And she got her wish, and ours, to live to see Elissa and Eric have children, precious Sienna and sweet Zachy. As recently as Passover, we were all together for the first seder, just the way she liked it.

There are a couple of things that will always stay with me about Grandma. From day one, Zeide and Grandma made me feel so much a part of the family. The first time I met them was on their 25th wedding anniversary. They were so warm and inviting. She would always introduce me to people as her daughter. That's how it was between us; that's how she made me feel. With her passing, I feel that gaping hole. She was the last of our parents. In my mind, as long as we had her, we still had Zeide, too, and in some way, my parents also. After all, she and Zeide were very close to my parents, and though they were 20 years apart in age, always shared an easy rapport and mutual respect. Grandma always kept their memory alive by talking about them and how much she loved them. Those of you who know me can appreciate how happy that made me!

To all those who are here to honor our beloved mother and grandmother, aunt, sister and friend, I thank you. To Erv and Brenda, who cared for her through all the years, through countless trips to doctors, to coordinating everything for her care and comfort, to giving her respect and devotion, I know how loved she felt. She will be remembered always.

I love you, Grandma. Rest in peace.

Brenda's Eulogy

It is hard to know what to say. How do you sum up a life? How do you sum up the complicated relationship of a mother and daughter?

I can't.

I will miss her!

I will miss her compliments: "Why don't you get a haircut?"

"Why don't you color your hair?"

I will miss her concern: "Do you have parking by your house?"

"Go home. Don't drive in the dark."

I will miss her endless questions about everyone I ever met: "Do you hear from Debbie Levy?"

"What about Stephanie?"

"No, Mom—I haven't heard from them since 12th grade."

Then she would move on to my college friends: "How is Bonnie? Her sister? Do you talk to Barbara? How is Eva? And Gail?"

She asked about new friends in Brooklyn that she didn't know well or never met.

My friends all liked her. I wondered why.

What did they talk to her about? Did she compliment them, too?

In Florida she'd go out to the screened-in porch and read a book. She always read—English, French, biographies, romance novels, history books. She would look out at the boats on the bay and talk for hours to my friends who came down with me for a visit. Years later she sat on the porch with Sam for hours— talking to a 2-,4-, 6-year-old.

Then there is Toby, who had a special relationship with my parents. She lives in California, but anytime she was in New York or Florida, she spent time with my parents. In fact, she was here last week for a visit; she flew back to California Saturday, and on Monday got right back on a plane to get here and pay her respects.

And there are Suri and Zelda, neighbors who live across the street and kept an eye on our mom and the house.

Thank you!

Our House 150-53 77th Road...50 years in one place. I never wanted that; I kept moving, kept switching relationships, jobs, furniture, homes.

I realized why when my father died, and it's even more crystal-clear now.

I could move around. I could change my life. Get married. Get divorced. Get married. Get divorced. And the truth is in the worst of times...there were no questions. No explanations required. Just—What do you need?

I could be me, because I had them.

A strong foundation. A great example. Endless love (compliments and concerns).

Love: My mother loved her family, her friends, her home, her life. She really loved her grandchildren. They were the best thing that ever happened to her. And to me.

Finally, after 20-plus years, there were younger people to ask the four questions on Passover. Other people she could focus on, so I could be a college student and get in and out of trouble that she never knew about because Elissa and Eric were her focus...and then finally, Sam. She always asked about Sam.

She enjoyed our weekly visits. Sam and I would watch The Bachelor with her, and America's Funniest Videos.

The last few years, she was less mobile, less social, read less...but always alert. She would rally and came alive when people would visit, or when we went out to breakfast.

I almost called her yesterday. Then I remembered she was no longer there. But I will always have that huge oil painting of her in the living room. I am sure I will continue to hear her voice: "How is Sam? . . . When will you color your hair?"

I love you, Mom!

Elissa's Eulogy

I am really lucky because when I think about my grandma I have so many memories to choose from all stages of my life. We had a special relationship and I know that she loved me so much and loved Ben and Zach so much. I hope that she knew how much we all loved her and looked up to her.

One of my favorite memories was sleeping over at Grandma's house. Eric didn't like to stay over as much—and as Grandma would often remind us, he would never stay over without me. But I was the brave one who would relish my weekends with her. And not just because she would make sure the house was stocked with sugary cereals and take us to McDonald's Playground. Grandma was the one who introduced me to some of my favorite TV shows as a kid. She was the one who watched Full House and Who's the

Boss? and when I came over, we watched them together and ate ice cream. It was a pretty simple evening but it was really special to us. We were pals, and over the past few years, Grandma would often ask me if I remember those times. I always told her I did and I always will.

When we were a little older, Eric and I started to go to Florida to visit Grandma and Zeide. Though it was only one year before our parents caught on to how much fun we had and started tagging along with us. During our first trip I remember how jam-packed Grandma's social calendar was. She had friends and family over all the time and would take us to see people and go to fun places. We would always take one long walk to go to a movie, and that tradition continued when I went to Florida to visit her and Zeide as an adult.

On one of those visits, Grandma invited me to go to a Holocaust memorial exhibit with her and Zeide. They were dedicating a railroad car that took Jews to the concentration camps, and there was a ceremony to display it. My priorities as a 20-something were more in line with getting a good tan, but while I was there, I instantly appreciated that I got to share that moment with her and Zeide. She told me that it was good for me to go as a member of the next generation, and I know that it was special to her that I was there. I will never forget that I am the descendant of Holocaust survivors and will make sure that I share our family's history with the next generation.

Which brings me to Zachary William, the baby I got pregnant with shortly after his namesake, my Zeide, passed away. I remember how excited I was to tell Grandma that I was pregnant. I knew she would be so happy to hear the news, and I hoped that it would give her a reason to stick around a while longer. She used the milestones in my life and Eric's life as goals for herself, and she had made it to both of our weddings and the birth of Eric's child. When I told her that I was pregnant, she told me that she wanted to meet my baby. And I told her I really wanted that, too. That I needed her to be around for the baby's birth. I am so happy that she met that goal. I am so lucky that she got to see me with my family and to light up when my son smiled at her. Over these past seven months, I have seen how much Zach's grandparents love him, and it only deepens my love and relationship with them. It makes me appreciate the love of a grandparent in a new way also and makes me appreciate that I had the very best.

Grandma, you will always be in my heart and I will miss you so much. You lived for your family and took such good care of us. You had a wicked sense of humor and you were easy to talk to. You were fun and energetic and loved to dance. You danced with me to The King and I record when I was 3 years old and you danced at my wedding when I was in my 30s. You were my pal. I will think of you every Mother's Day, wishing you were here on Earth with us but taking comfort in the fact that you are with Zeide and watching over us.

Eric's Eulogy

Queen Esther: So brave, and so lovely. While I wish I could take credit for these poetic words, they actually come from a children's book called Purim Masquerade that my 2-year-old daughter, Sienna, is quite fond of. We often read that book, and I always tried to tell Sienna that "Esther" was the name of my Grandma, and her Babi.

And those two adjectives—brave and lovely—are a great way

to describe my grandma.

So brave describes her courageous side. It describes her fighting side. Her perseverance.

This is a woman that was able to hide from and escape the Nazis and, as a 12-year-old, take care of her two younger siblings—without having her own mom by her side.

This was a woman who came to the U.S. and made a full life for herself and her family.

This was a woman who fought through cancer for 20-plus years. She kept fighting. She never gave in. She fought to make sure she saw Sammy be born. She fought to make sure she saw me and Elissa get married. And she fought to make sure that she got to meet her great-grandchildren, Sienna and Zach.

Sienna got to know her Babi. At Passover this year in Plainview, Grandma walked around the house with the help of her walker. A few days later, Sienna was using the little step stool in our kitchen as a walker and saying "like Babi." I was amazed. It melted my heart that she picked up on that. And just the other day when Jess and I were showing her pictures from our wedding day, she pointed to my Grandma and said, "Babi." She knew her. I'll always cherish that.

My dad always reminded me that she and Zeide were fighters. They survived, and they kept fighting. He reminded me of this because he wanted me to always know—especially in tough times—that I had that "fighter's" blood running through me. And now Sienna and Zach have it running through them. I'll be sure to remind Sienna of this, so she knows where it comes from.

So lovely describes my Grandma's giving, loving and caring side. It describes how she opened up her home and her heart, not only to her family, but to her friends as well as anyone else that came in her path. I always remember Aunt Brenda saying that her friends always really enjoyed talking with Grandma. Grandma and Zeide had a ton of friends, and I got to see that first-hand in Flushing and Florida.

I got to see how warm and welcoming she was to Jess when she first met her. She instantly made her feel like she was a part of the family. Every time I called, she always asked: "How's Jessie? How are her parents? How's her brother? They're good people."

She wanted to know that everybody was OK. In the last couple years, any time I called, I was off the phone in two minutes. She wanted to know how I was doing, how Jessie was doing, how Sienna was doing, and how the family was doing. If I told her that everybody was doing well, and we were seeing each other soon, she was content. That was the end of the conversation. I'd ask her how she was doing but she never wanted to complain to me. She'd say, "Comme ci, comme ca," or "There are good days and bad days." She just wanted to hear my voice and hear that everybody was OK. "That's the most important thing," she would always say.

And the "Queen" in "Queen Esther" refers to the fact that in many ways she is the matriarch of the Farkas family. She was the one we all looked up to, and who hosted and cooked for us for so many years. I have fantastic memories of her and Zeide. From visiting them down in Florida, where we hung out by the pool and went for walks around North Miami Beach, to the countless Jewish holidays spent running around their house, and underneath their table, to sleeping over their house—often on the floor next to their bed or snuggled up between them in the crack of their two single beds pushed together. I remember them spoiling me with soda, Trix cereal, and trips to McDonald's Playground and the movies.

Most of all, I remember all the love she put out into the world that was geared my way. I loved her very much, I'm thankful that I got to spend 30-plus years with her and I trust that she knew how much I loved her—even though she always teased me about being afraid to sleep over their house the first time my parents tried leaving me with them.

I'm glad she's no longer in pain, and that she's with Zeide looking down at all they've helped to create.

I love you, Grandma!

Bibliography

Print Sources

Berger, Anna. *Munkács: A World That Was*. Thesis: Department of Hebrew, Biblical and Jewish Studies. The University of Sydney, July, 2008.

Decostes, Charlotte. *Jewish Hidden Children in Belgium During the Holocaust: A Comparative Study of Their Hiding Places at Christian Establishments, Private Families, and Jewish Orphanages*. Thesis for University of North Texas, December, 2006.

Frankl, Viktor E. *Man's Search for Meaning*. Simon & Schuster, 1963.

Helmreich, William B. *Against All Odds: Holocaust Survivors and the Successful Lives They Made in America*. Simon & Schuster, 1992.

Honey, Michael. *Research Notes on the Hungarian Holocaust: We Remember the Holocaust of Hungarian Jewry*. http://zchor.org, 2008.

Rubin, Debra. "When Nuns Helped Rescue Jewish Children." *New Jersey Jewish News*, May 2014.

Segal, Raz. *Days of Ruin: Jews of Munkacz During the Holocaust*. Yad Vashem, 2016.

Shik, Na'ama. *Women in Auschwitz:* Yad Vashem, On the Holocaust Podcast. Yad Vashem.

Viran, Karen. *Uzhgorod: Memorial Places of Jewish History* Translated by Tibor Weitzner.

Vromen, Suzanne. *Hidden Children of the Holocaust: Belgian Nuns and Their Daring Rescue of Young Jews from the Nazis*. Oxford University Press, 2008.

Tapes

Farkas, Esther. Stephen Spielberg Shoah Foundation Tape, Interview code-16462. Queens, New York, June 24, 1996.

Farkas, Moritz. Stephen Spielberg Shoah Foundation Tape. Interview code-23721. Moselle, France, December 3, 1996.

Farkas, Samuel. Audiotapes recorded in Queens, New York, April 1979.

Farkas, Wilhelm. Stephen Spielberg Shoah Foundation Tape. Interview code-16439. Queens, New York, June 24, 1996.

Websites

archwum@auschwitz.org

JewishGen.org The JewishGen Hungary Database

JewishGen.org The JewishGen Ukraine Database

jewishGen.org KahilaLinks

Acknowledgments

Researching and writing this book was a formidable undertaking and could not have been completed without the encouragement and help provided by numerous friends and family members. The project began after my parents passed away a few years ago, at which point our two children, Elissa and Eric, were struck by the fact that they no longer had any grandparents around. Both of them and my sister, Brenda, had always encouraged Sue and me to write our family stories. Now, Elissa and Eric were encouraging us again, although I felt I still had a bit of time to get started. But the Covid pandemic and the lockdown that followed, and my own medical diagnosis of lymphoma, made it feel like the universe was sending me a message: The book needed to be written. And like most projects I have thrown myself into, once I began researching my family history and then writing each chapter, it became what I wanted and needed to do.

I want to thank three dear and long time friends—Harvey Simon, Lynne Hanner Milgram and John Iorio—for reading the earliest version of the book and providing me with their enthusiastic reactions and helpful suggestions. I also want to thank Peggy Intrator, a friend for 50 years, for viewing my Uncle Moishe's Shoah Foundation tape and translating it from French to English with her copious and invaluable notes.

Nanette Girolamo, who has been making all of my articles and reports read better since we worked together in the Bethpage School District, edited the first draft of the book. Her knowledge of grammar and usage is outstanding. In addition, she and her husband,

Paul, cheered me on as well.

I have to thank Jay Schreiber, another longtime friend who was an editor at the *New York Times* for close to 30 years. He tirelessly read and reread every word of this book and made corrections and suggestions that were invaluable and made this book much better.

I also want to acknowledge Elissa and Eric, who not only pushed me to write this book but were supportive and enthusiastic all the way through this process.

And I want to thank my wife, Sue, for her unwavering interest, enthusiasm and support—not just in the writing of this book but throughout our lives together. She helped me with indispensable advice and urged me to tell more rather than less, which is often my tendency. She loved my parents and wanted their story to reflect how much she and we loved them and why.

I want to acknowledge our grandchildren—Sienna, Zachy, Ruby and Zoe—who continually amaze us and make us want to be the best versions of ourselves. Their enthusiasm for life and their love would indeed make their great-grandparents proud. This book is my parents' story, our story and their story.

Finally, I want to thank my parents for living a life of love and meaning where all of us felt loved. This is my tribute to them.

www.ingramcontent.com/pod-product-compliance
Lightning Source LLC
Chambersburg PA
CBHW031625160426
43196CB00006B/283